Honeysuckle Sipping

Honeysuckle Sipping

The Plant Lore of Childhood

By Jeanné R. Chesanow

Illustrated by
Norma Cuneo

Down East Books

ISBN 0-89272-234-7

Grateful acknowledgment is made for permission to quote from the following:

Open Horizons, by Sigurd F. Olson. Copyright © 1969 by Sigurd F. Olson. Reprinted by permission of Alfred E. Knopf, Inc.

From Two to Five, by Kornei Chukovsky, translated and edited by Miriam Morton. This translation © 1963 by Miriam Morton. Reprinted by permission of the University of California Press

Home Ground: A Gardener's Miscellany, by Allen Lacy. Copyright © 1984 by Allen Lacy. Reprinted by permission of Farrar, Straus & Giroux, Inc.

Ohio Town, by Helen Hooven Santmyer (pps. 278, 279, 280, 286, 287, 293). Copyright © 1956, 1961, 1962 by the Ohio State University Press. Reprinted by permission of Harper & Row Publishers, Inc.

"Reflections of a Reluctant Gardener," by V.S. Naipaul, in *House & Garden,* Jan. 1986. Reprinted courtesy of House & Garden, copyright © 1986 by The Conde Nast Publications, Inc.

Library of Congress Catalog Card Number 87-51122
Cover design by Dawn Peterson
Printed at Hamilton Printing Co., Renssalaer, N.Y.

4 5 3

Down East Books, P.O. Box 679
Camden, ME 04843

Contents

The plants that are closest to you are
those from your childhood;
those are the ones you truly love . . .

— V.S. Naipaul

To all who remember
the plants from their childhoods.

Preface

IN THE SPRING OF 1984, as I was reading Allen Lacy's *Home Ground*, a passage in the chapter "A Damnable Vine's Sweet Ambrosia" caught my attention. The "damnable vine" was honeysuckle, whose "sweet ambrosia" is savored by the *cognoscenti*. Having mastered the art of honeysuckle sipping early in life, Lacy wanted to make sure his sons did not miss out on that special magic. When he took the boys out to demonstrate, he discovered they already knew the secret of the honeysuckle. Lacy commented that there is a body of knowledge that children learn on their own.

The passage evoked bits of lore that I had "just known" as a child — buttercups under the chin, picking petals from daisies, and wishing on dandelion seedheads. I asked friends about their childhood plant lore and began to scour the literature for more material. With a book taking shape in my mind (a compilation of children's plant lore), I placed a query in the September issue of *Gardens for All* (now *National Gardening*) asking for "anything you can remember from childhood having to do with plants — games, stories, rhymes, imaginative uses for plants, customs such as petal-pulling, and activities like making horse chestnut rings."

Twenty-two people from all over the country wrote, reminiscing about hollyhock dolls, bubble pipes made from squash stems, and battles with horse chestnuts.

I combined these letters with additional material into a fifty-four-page booklet, *Honeysuckle Sipping,* which I sent out to the contributors, to friends, and to fellow gardeners. Their enthusiastic responses encouraged me to expand the manuscript. A second request in the January 1985 *Gardens for All* garnered twenty-five more letters; the writers' childhoods spanned every decade of the twentieth century from the teens to the sixties.

More letters came in response to an article, "Honeysuckle Sipping," in the summer 1986 issue of *Pacific Horticulture.* When Joan Paulson Gage mentioned my plant lore study in her column "Kids in the Country" (*Country Living,* September 1986), 210 letters arrived, many in time to be included in the final version of the manuscript (the rest saved for the next volume). At the time of the last draft, the contributions were from forty-three states, Canada, France, England, and Sweden. The letters are the heart of the book — recollections of childhood pastimes, told with obvious joy.

The rest of the book is based on library research done in 1985 and 1986. The subject matter proved elusive enough to satisfy even a Jessica Fletcher. I learned to sniff out traces of children's plant lore from books in several categories, and the most informative ones are listed in the Bibliography. A thick 1880s book of plant lore might contain one paragraph or two about children's customs. Writers of wildflower guide books occasionally remarked on a childhood diversion; nature writer/philosophers like Teale and Borland were a source of inspiration as well as a few notes on children's pastimes. (Borland's *Book of Days* has as its May 1 entry a wonderful description of May Day in New England fifty years ago.) Books on children's games yielded up a number of plant games and pastimes from both England and the United States. Tucked away in biographies and novels were bits of long-remembered plant lore. Margaret Truman, for example, sailed walnut-shell boats in her grandmother's back yard. Margaret Mead, early on dewy summer mornings in New Hampshire, showed her daughter Catherine (Bateson) the fairies' tablecloths (dew-covered spider webs) and fairy roses (red lichens) and told her stories of a king and queen who ruled a secret kingdom down among the grass stems of the meadow. Catherine's father, on the other hand, taught her Latin names for plants and explained that daisies could be used for the "He loves me; he loves me not" predictions because the "petals" are actually flowerets, which vary in number.

Of the books on toys and child development, the Newsons' most closely expressed the ideas put forth in *Honeysuckle Sipping.* Since play is

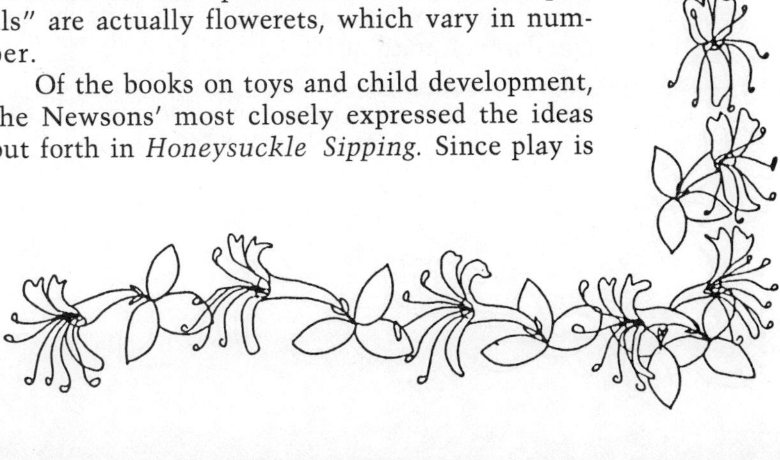

primary and toys merely the props, children create toys if they have none — a stick doll, a vine swing, a bamboo cane. Play is the leaping-off point for creative thinking and invention. Natural materials are toys par excellence because they leave much to the imagination. They also appeal to the senses; imagine a whistle made from persimmon or sassafras, woods chosen because they smell and taste good!

Each plant used for play was known by the season in which it appeared and treasured for that brief time. For example, milkweed silk is moist and malleable (for shaping into toys) for only a short time before it emerges as fluff and becomes a different form of amusement.

It would have been unsatisfying to simply enumerate each custom or game without conveying a sense of the accompanying mood or sensation. Virtually every letter writer recalled her (or his) pastimes with happiness, telling of textures, smells, the sense of adventure, the spirit inherent in the play. *Honeysuckle Sipping* follows a century of children through a year, four seasons of play with and among plants.

Welcome to the plant world of children. Within this charmed circle of honeysuckle sippers, you may find a part of yourself that has lain dormant until now.

J.R. Chesanow, Cheshire, Conn.
September 1987

Acknowledgments

THANK YOU TO ALL who wrote down your plant memories. This book is yours.

My special thanks to a few people who made special contributions: Bob Burrell, who sent a photo of his daughter; Hilda Badger Drummond, who loaned me her precious set of peach and cherry pit baskets; Ann James van Hooser, who sketched hollyhock dolls and leaf forts; Blanche Farthing, who showed me the star in the cottonwood; Jean Rosenfeld, who sent me the filaree seeds. Thanks also to Alice Betz and Elizabeth Pentecost for their sketches, and to Norman Singer, Geoff Charlesworth, and George Waters for their encouragement.

Joan Paulson Gage helped in getting the material seen by many people, and the librarians at Cheshire (Connecticut) Library were very helpful too, especially in getting the Folkard book. My sons, Andrei and Matt, always knew I could write the book; my mother wrote contributions and deserves extra thanks for her support. And, as always, Ches was standing by.

Martha Brown helped compile the plant list and Lillian Chesanow sent valuable clippings.

Since this is a book about children I need to thank several children for their help: Valerie

Atwell (age eight) wrote me a delightful letter telling how she plays with plants; Carrie, Crista, and Tammy Wolak visited my garden and posed for photographs.

Thanks to Helen Bedard, who did my typing from less-than-perfect drafts, to Betty Vigneron for the information on witch hazel seeds, and to Mary Knapp for the materials she sent.

I am grateful to Evelyn Vincent for allowing me to use excerpts from her unpublished novel, *No Plantations.*

Thank you to Tam Mossman for your interest and encouragement, to Melody Smith for sending me the *Country Living* clipping, and to Pat Talbert, who showed my little book to W.G. Waters.

Sandy Bayes has alerted the Waynesville, Ohio, area to the publication of this book; hurrah for her!

Finally, I extend sincere appreciation to my judicious and unflappable editor, Karin Womer, who orchestrated the whole project.

Introduction

FOR CENTURIES children have amused themselves with the leaves, roots, flowers, stems, and fruits of plants. Games with nuts, dating from ancient Greece and Rome, are perhaps the oldest recorded tradition of plant play. Nut games were such an integral part of a Roman boy's childhood that the expression *nuces relinquere* took on the meaning "to put aside childish things." One such game was orca (?), in which boys pitched nuts into a jar (an *orca*) or a shallow pit scooped out of the ground; in ancient Greece this game's arena was a circle drawn in the dirt. Nuts that landed outside the target were forfeited. (During the 1800s on the streets of New York, boys played similar games with marbles, buttons, or cherry pits.)

Jean Froissart (1338-1410?), the French poet who chronicled his life in verse, lists Nuts as one of the games he played during his boyhood.[1] In "L'Espinette Amoureuse" (the section of the *Chronicle* devoted to his youth) Froissart also mentioned *erbelette* (grass), which is possibly a reference to the custom of drawing straws (or stalks of grass) to determine who will go first in a game, or who will be *It.* Still done today, often with toothpicks, this tradition dic-

tates that the person who draws the shortest "straw" is the loser and must abide by some previously set condition. *Erbelette* could also refer to the practice of picking tufts from various grasses to find out whether "She loves me" or "loves me not." This children's custom, still practiced today (more commonly with daisy petals), was evidently well established by the Middle Ages, since the German poet Walther von der Vogelweide (1170-1230) wrote:

A spire of grass has made me gay —
I measured in the self-same way
I have seen practiced by a child,
Come look and listen if she really does,
She does, does not, she does, does not,
she does!

A third medieval poem, *Histoire de Guillaume de Maréchal* (author unknown) describes a plantain duel that took place in 1219. (Versions of this game are still played in England today.)[2] The poem is about William Marshal, Regent of England, who, as a boy, was held hostage in King Stephen's camp during the siege of Newbury. One day in Stephen's tent, William challenged the king to a plaintain duel, a contest in which each of two players is armed with a narrow-leaved plantain stalk and flower head. The combatants spar with the stalks until one plantain is decapitated; in a set number of duels the winner is the one who accumulates the most flower heads. In the poem young William took first turn and beheaded the king's "knight."

In the sixteenth- and seventeenth-century herbals there are a few passing references to children's uses of plants. For example, John Gerard (1545-1612) in his *Herball* (first published in 1597) noted: "Children with delight make chains and pretty gewgaws of the fruit of roses."

The nineteenth century brought a surge of interest in folklore; societies were formed in England and America to study and record folk customs of all kinds, including plant lore. In the 1880s a number of books on plant lore were published, including Richard Folkard's book with the all-encompassing title *Plant Lore, Legend and Lyrics: Embracing the Myths, Traditions, Superstitions, and Folk-Lore of the Plant Kingdom.* The Reverend Thistleton-Dyer devoted one chapter in his *Folk-Lore of Plants* (1889) to (English) children's customs, including telling time by blowing on a dandelion seedhead — a practice passed along to American children. Alice Morse Earle described American children's flower lore of the 1850s in one chapter of her book, *Child Life in Colonial Days* (1899). (The remainder of the book was concerned with childhood during the Colonial period, but "The Flower Lore of Children" was an account of the author's own girlhood.) Fanny Bergen's *Animal and Plant Lore* (1899), published by the American Folklore Society, included a few children's customs and rhymes. In *La Flore* (volume 6 of his *Folklore de France*) Paul Sébillot presented a

wealth of detail on plant lore, including children's games, homemade toys, pranks, rhymes and superstitions (all largely from Brittany, Sébillot's native province). First published from 1904 to 1906, Sébillot's book describes lore of the 1800s (with some materials dating as far back as the fourteenth century); many of the same children's customs have been observed also in England and in the United States.

Studies of children's games, also part of the nineteenth-century enthusiam for folklore, included such plant games as Violet Roosters and Poppy Shows. Both games appear in Alice Gomme's *Traditional Games of England, Scotland, and Ireland* (1889) and in William Wells Newell's *Games and Songs of American Children* (1883). In the twentieth century, Iona and Peter Opie meticulously combed earlier sources and interviewed English children to write their *Lore and Language of Schoolchildren* (1959) and *Children's Games in Street and Playground* (1969). (Many of the children they studied were still playing the games described by Gomme.) Brian Sutton-Smith (1972) reported on a century of children's games (1840-1950) in New Zealand; American folklorists like Carl Withers, Duncan Emrich, and Mary and Herbert Knapp documented various aspects of twentieth-century children's lore.

Polls of urban American children (taken in 1890, 1937, and 1959) asking them to rank their preferences in games, showed that pastimes with seeds, nuts, flowers, and leaves were near the top of the list in 1890 but had disappeared from the list by 1959. Many children, however, continued to play with plant materials in both traditional and innovative ways. Their plant lore recollections (1915-1986), combined with earlier references, are the foundation of this book.

The spot of earth where we [are] born
[makes] such a difference to us . . .
these gray ledges hold me by the roots,
as they do the bayberry bushes,
the sweet-fern, and the rock saxifrage.

— Lucy Larcom, 1889

SPRING

Sailing Ships

IN SPRING, children burst with an exuberance that cannot be contained. Their elders try to tame them, but their spirits are high, tuned to the celebration of the new season. The weather may be gray and raw, but every day brings fresh evidence of spring's nearness. Children make boats out of anything that comes to hand — sticks, leaves, seed pods — and set them to sail. This ancient pastime, enjoyed by Greek children 2300 years ago, was also part of Jean Froissart's childhood in the Middle Ages. He wrote:

In that early childish day
I was never tired to play
Games that children every one
Love until twelve years are done
To dam up a rivulet
With a small tile or else to let
A small saucer for a boat
Down the purling gutter float:
Over two bricks at our will
To erect a water mill:
And in the end wash clean from dirt,
In the streamlet, cap and shirt.
We have heart and eye together
To see scud a sailing feather.

Long after Froissart wrote this *Chronicle,* children still sailed ships. In the late 1850s, Alice Morse Earle, growing up in Worcester, Massachusetts, made elaborate boats from the

leaves of flower de luce (iris) and filled them with bright flower passengers:

What . . . quaint antique-shaped boats with swelling lateen sail and pennant of striped grass could be made from the flat, sword-like leaves of the flower de luce! Filled with flowers, these leafy boats could be set adrift down a tiny brook in the meadow or . . . the purling gutter of a hill-side street. The flowers chosen to sail in these tiny crafts were those most human of all flowers — pansies, or their smallest garden sisters, the ladies' delights [johnny-jump-ups, Viola tricolor hortensis*], that turned their happy faces to us from every nook and corner of the garden.*

In Tuscumbia, Missouri, in the 1940s Terra Joann Waters and her brother pursued this same sport on their grandparents' farm. She recalls:

Nothing was as much fun as sailing acorns and other objects on a leaf down the creek. What imaginative stories our minds would conjure up to go along with our sailing ships!

In a similar pastime, Chippewa[1] children folded cattail leaves, origami fashion, to make ducks. They put flocks of these green birds into the water and watched them bob away on the swift current.

Schooldays, Schooldays . . .

It was the pussy willows that convinced our teachers that spring was on the way. When they saw the furry catkins that we had picked and

brought into the school, they relaxed into smiles. We could tell they were as happy as we were — they almost enjoyed recess duty, dawdling a bit before shooing us back inside. Invariably our art lesson for that day would be to draw pussy willows, using as our model the branches in the jar of water high on the window sill. Our formula never varied — gray or brown crayon stems and white chalk catkins on a background of blue construction paper. (J. Stewart, Great Barrington, Massachusetts, 1940s.)

Some children knew how to make a row of cats on a fence by gluing three or four catkins on a piece of paper, then drawing a fence and tails hanging down from the little cats.

Nineteenth-century children had hailed the arrival of the pussy willows by calling excitedly to one another, "Pussy willows are out!" Alice Morse Earle explains why this plant brought such joy:

The earliest sign of spring in the fields and woods in my childhood was the appearance of the willow catkins . . . After the snow, the whiteness, and the chill of a New England winter, how eagerly we turned to pussy willows as a promise of summer and sunshine.

Lila Ritter, as a little girl in rural Kentucky in the 1920s, was told that pussy willows were good to have around because they might turn into kittens. An old Polish legend[2] explains the relationship between pussy willows and kittens:

Once upon a time, very long ago, there were

no pussy willows. There were willow trees, but they had no catkins in the spring. In a place far away, there was a beautiful, smoothly flowing river with tall willows growing along its edges. One day a man carrying a sack came to the river. A large cat that was meowing sadly followed the man. This mother cat was crying because the man was going to drown her kittens. Sure enough, the man opened his sack and dumped the kittens into the water! But . . . just then the willow trees put down their long branches into the river. The kittens held on to the branches and were saved! Ever since then, in spring, willows have had buds as soft to the touch as a kitten's fur.

Early spring also meant skunk cabbages. First the purpley-red points of the flower buds poked up through the mud in woods and marshes. Later came the bright green leaves, which smelled only faintly of cabbage and not at all like skunk — unless they were either crushed or brought indoors. Then they stank! Every year someone brought a leaf to school for this prank, recalled by Bob Burrell from his 1940s boyhood in western Ohio:

A dirty trick to play on someone who didn't know wildflowers was to give them a big leaf from a skunk cabbage and have them crumple it back and forth in their hands and then smell them.

Since the skunky odor lasted for quite a while, the victim was usually relegated to the hallway. Classmates walking by couldn't resist making comments or holding their noses.

Another recollection of skunk cabbage comes from George Schenk, the noted gardener and writer. In his book, *The Complete Shade Gardener*, Schenk tells how he and his brother admired the yellow flame-shaped flowers of *Lysichitum americanum*, the western skunk cabbage, which grew near their Oregon home. The boys had picked a bouquet of these flowers and had tried twice to bring it into the house only to be told to remove it. Parental disapproval of course made the flowers irresistible, so they sneaked the bouquet into the basement. Within a short time an unmistakable odor drifted up into the living room where the grownups were sitting. Back down came WORDS — the flowers were out of the house in short order!

Later in the spring appeared jack-in-the-pulpit, with its distinctive green spadix (the

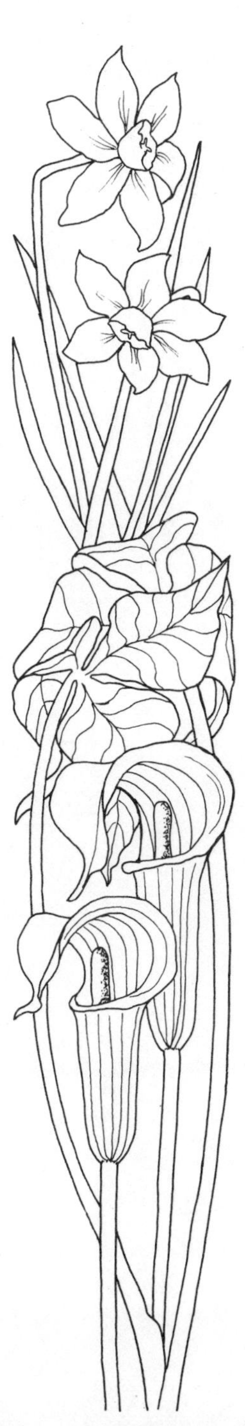

preacher) under a green- or purple-striped spathe (the pulpit). Children boasted that they could make Jack preach; they squeezed the plant at the base of the spathe to make a squeaking sound. Other names for jack-in-the-pulpit are dragon root and memory root. Both names seem appropriate to anyone who has ever had the following trick played on him. A boy who knew plants would dig up a corm of memory root, bring it to school, and dare another boy to take a bite. A tiny piece on one's tongue is as fiery as a dragon's breath, and remains fixed in memory for all time!

Jenilu Richie, who grew up in Memphis, Tennessee, in the 1940s, remembers that some of the girls in her class would bring the first jonquils of spring to school and put them in their inkwells.[3] After sitting in the blue ink for a day, the stems had turned blue. By the second day, the whole flower was veined in blue, and if left until the third day, the whole jonquil would be stained indigo. Students were not the only ones who transformed jonquils:

The teacher kept a bottle of red ink on her desk for marking papers. If she were an especially nice teacher she would permit a jonquil to sit in her red-ink bottle. Every day we would look at . . . how the color had changed.

When the lilacs came into bloom, girls carried fragrant bunches to school, as Alice Morse

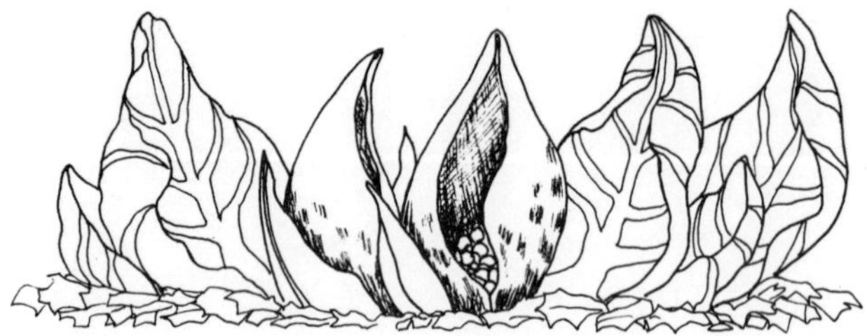

Earle recalls: *"A bunch of lilacs was ever a favorite gift for 'teacher,' to be placed in a broken-nosed pitcher on her desk."*

After their schoolwork was finished, Alice and some of the girls made lilac wreaths. On a piece of colored paper they made a circle by pushing one lilac floret into another. The petals stuck together without glue.

The alternation of color in these wreaths — ([or example] one white and two purple lilac petals . . .— could easily prove the ingenuity and originality of the child who produced them .

To make lilac bracelets or necklaces, the girls strung the florets together with needle and thread. If a girl found a "luck lilac" among the florets, she could use it to tell if a certain boy loved her. According to Alice Morse Earle, who did this in the 1860s:

There will occasionally appear a tiny lilac flower, usually a white lilac, with five divisions of the petal instead of four — this is a Luck Lilac.[4] *It must be solemnly swallowed. If it goes down smoothly, the dabbler in magic cries out, "He loves me!" If she chokes on her floral food, she must say sadly, "He loves me not." I remember once calling out with gratification and pride, "He loves me!" "Who is he?" asked my older companion. "Oh, I didn't know he had to be somebody," I answered in surprise, to be met with derisive laughter at my satisfaction with a lover in general and not in particular. It was a matter of Lilac-Luck etiquette that the lover's*

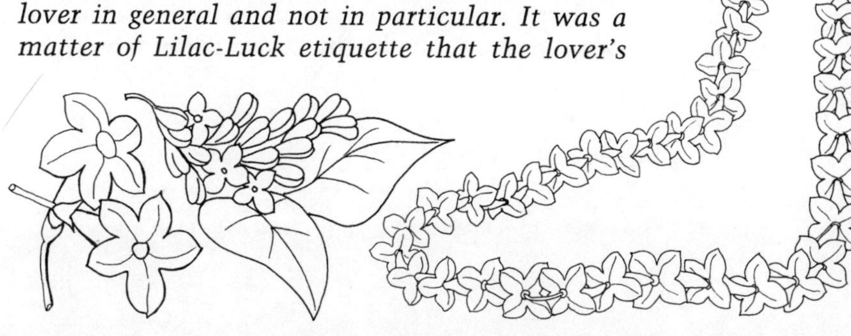

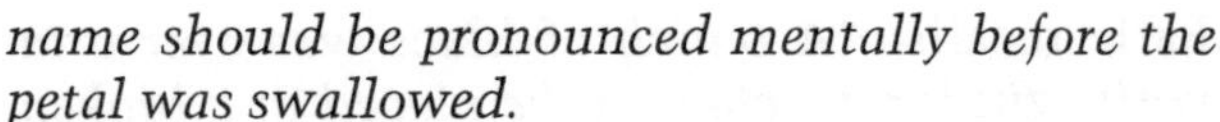

name should be pronounced mentally before the petal was swallowed.

At recess the children ran outside, eager to be in the spring air. They played the same games that ancient Greek children had: hopscotch, jump rope, marbles, jacks, and tag. One of the favorite kinds of tag was Wood Tag or Poison Oak. Frances Lehde and her friends often played it during the 1920s in Kentucky:

The safe base for everyone except the kid who was "it" was anyplace where we could touch wood[5] *— the corner of a building, a fence post, a tree, a bush, or even a piece of bark, a limb, or a board lying on the ground. Any piece of wood lying on the ground had to be large enough to be visible on both sides of one's foot, and could not be moved by hand but could be nudged by a foot. On a tree, one hand touching it was enough. When the person who was "it" yelled "Poison Oak!" everyone had to change bases and find safety by touching wood before being tagged. Of course very often two kids would head for the same tree or post and one or the other had to change course. The "it," or "chaser," always had to be alert to such changes. If you were tagged you became the new "it" and had to try to tag the old "it" before he or she reached safety.*

Jump rope was always fun, with either one or two ropes (double dutch). A dandelion jump rope

was surprisingly sturdy; these were made by tying slip knots to the stems of two dandelions at a time. *"Sometimes the girls would play singing games like Farmer in the Dell, A Tisket A Tasket, London Bridge, and Go In and Out the Window."* (J. Stewart)

In southern Illinois, at a one-room school during the 1930s, the girls often climbed the wooded hill behind the school. There they would choose one girl as queen for the day, with the other girls to be her servants. Her Majesty dined on the rarer violet-flowered wood sorrel (*Oxalis violacea*) while her slaves had to be content with the common yellow-flowered variety (*Oxalis corniculata*). (Told to Nancy Sue Leske, of Anna, Illinois).

When the maple seed pods whirled down from the trees, they suggested many amusements. Grace Graham remembers:

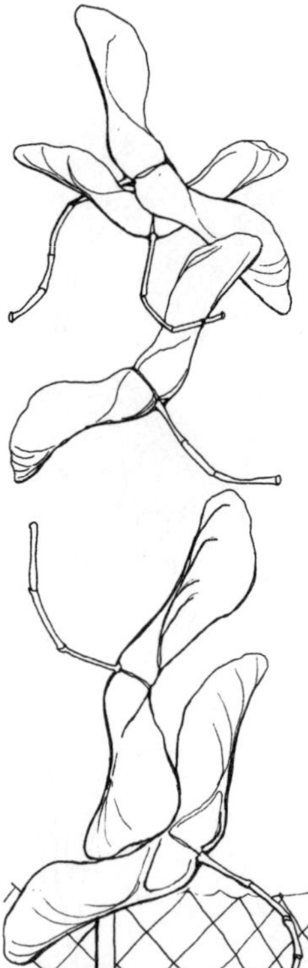

When I was a little girl growing up in Stoneham, Massachusetts, in the 1920s, there were two long rows of large maple trees on both sides of the long driveway leading to our house — maybe a dozen trees in all. In the springtime, when the trees began to drop their seeds, my girl friend and I would gather the pods while they were still green. We would pry open the full seed end and put them on our earlobes for make-believe earrings when we played house. Of course, my older brother used to tease us by putting the open end of the pod on the cartilage of his nose like a ring and chase us around like a cannibal!

And from Great Barrington, Massachusetts,

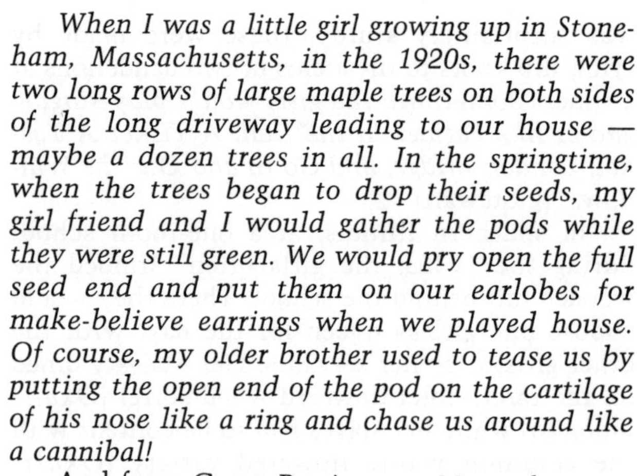

Marge Evans reports: "*We used to take the maple seeds, split the seed end, and stick them on the bridge of our nose, pretending they were glasses*" (1920s).

Twenty years later, children still used the pods as eyeglasses but also began to call them "whirlybirds." During World War II, helicopters became more common, and children noticed that half seed pods (especially the dried brown ones) rotated like a helicopter's blade. Holding the pods up high, they let the whirlybirds go and watched as they circled to the ground.[6]

A favorite pastime from coast to coast was Polly Noses (also called Noses, Pinocchio Noses, and Fairy Noses). Noses were made by

sticking half a green seed pod to your nose. Jean Morgan explains, *"We called these Polly Noses because they looked like a parrot's beak"* (Brooklyn, New York, 1930s). Running around to see whose nose would stay on the longest was fun. Eva Cohen (Oregon) also remembers sticking the half seed pods to her arms as feathers.

Most fun of all was the whistle that could be made with the tail of a maple seed (one wing with the seed ripped off). Melody Smith, who made these whistles in Marshfield, Wisconsin, in the 1950s explains: *"We took this tail, put it on top of our tongue with the thicker edge facing back, lifted it up behind our front teeth, and blew."*

Helen Hooven Santmyer, writing about her

home town of Xenia, in the book *Ohio Town*, elucidates further:

This could be done in school to upset procedure and annoy the teacher, because without the least contortion of your face beyond a slight parting of the lips, a whole range of noises could be produced from the merest suggestion of a sibilant whisper to a most appalling squawk. (early 1900s)

These same ingenious whistles could also be made from small leaves. Any leaf that was about one inch long and not more than half an inch wide was suitable. The stem end faced up, held fast by the tongue, while the soft part hung down, where it vibrated with every breath. Some

kids had the knack of making these noisemakers by tearing a squarish piece out of the side of a large dandelion leaf. This squawker was held in one's mouth just as the other leaves or seeds were. Depending on the skill of the musician, the sound could vary from a slight whistling to an alarming screech. A favorite prank was to pretend to blow your nose into a large handkerchief while actually blowing through the hidden noisemaker. The raucous sound that came forth was as obnoxious as W.C. Fields's infamous raspberries.

With a dandelion stem anyone could be a horn player,[7] blatting and wailing all the way home from school. It took a knack to play these horns, but they were easy to make. The very long stems (twelve to sixteen inches), usually found growing in uncut roadside grasses, made the best instruments. After making a quarter-inch slit in the narrower end, the musician put this part in his mouth and blew. The two little flaps vibrated, creating a variety of sounds. Horns of different lengths produced tones of varying pitch; the longer the stem, the deeper the note. Some kids put holes along the side of the stem and played different notes by covering up various combinations of holes. The effect of a group of dandelion trumpeters could be overwhelming — a caterwauling chorus giving notice that school was out!

On nice days we changed out of our school clothes, had a snack, and headed outdoors as fast as we could. We were overflowing with young energy, and the spring gardens, woods, and fields promised us hours of pleasure. (J. Stewart, 1940s.)

Springtime in the Garden

In the remembered gardens of spring, time passed quickly. Laughter and fantasy were the order of the day. To the small children who played there, it was a magic place where the plants became playhouses or props for games, and flowers seemed to have expressive faces.

From the first weeks of a baby's life, faces are the most fascinating objects in view; no wonder children find faces everywhere — in the contours of a fire hydrant, in the patterns of craters on the moon, and in blotches on a pansy. Pansies were the passengers on the iris-leaf ships because of their faces. Alice Morse Earle saw in the ladies' delights (johnny-jump-ups) . . . *[An] infinite variety of expression; some are laughing and roguish, some sharp and shrewd, some surprised, others worried, all are animated and vivacious, and a few saucy to a degree. They are as companionable as people — nay, more; they are as companionable as children. No wonder children love them; they recognize kindred spirits. I know a child who had stolen a choice rose and hidden it under her apron. But as she passed a bed of Ladies' Delights blowing in the wind, peering, winking, mocking, she sud-*

denly threw the rose at them, crying out pettishly, "Here! take your old flower!"

Some children used pansies as paper dolls, spreading them on the grass and then dressing them in leaves and berries.

In addition to faces, entire human figures were found in the various parts of many flowers. For example, the center of a pansy contained an old man washing his feet, revealed when all the petals have been pulled from the flower. The storyteller pulls the petals off in a certain order to illustrate each step of the following story.

Once upon a time there was a man with two daughters. The man's wife had died, so he looked around for a new wife. He married a beautiful but very selfish woman with two ugly daughters. This new wife wanted her *daughters to wear beautiful clothes, but she made the man's daughters wear very plain clothes. These are the man's two daughters* (point to petals 1 and 2). *See, their gowns have no trimmings on them — just plain. She was so stingy she made those two girls sit on one chair* (tear off 1 and 2 and show, on the back of the flower, the single sepal that had supported the two petals). *Her own two daughters each had a pretty dress with decorations* (point to petals 3 and 4) *and each of them had her own chair* (tear off 3 and 4 and show that each had its own sepal). *To show you just how selfish this woman was, she had the fullest skirt of all, with the fanciest design* (point to 5). *And how many chairs do you think this woman kept for herself? Two!* (Tear off 5 to show two supporting sepals.)*Where was that poor man all this time? I'll show you* (carefully snip off the two sepals with your thumbnail). *She made him sit down in the basement with his feet in a pail of water. Do you see him? This is the little man, sitting in his chair with a piece of red flannel around his neck to keep him warm. He is soaking his feet in a tub. Do you want to see his legs?* (Snip open the "tub.")[8]

Such stories nourished the children's imaginations. Between the ages of two and six, childrens' inventiveness flourishes, often expressed in nonsensical words and verses or games of make-believe. The outdoors was a place where imagination could reign, and all sorts of legendary creatures — elves, mossmen, gnomes, and fairies — were part of the traditional lore of the garden.

Alice Betz, growing up in south St. Louis, Missouri, in the 1930s, imagined that fairies lived in her father's iris-filled garden and that one day she would hear them sing:

White coral bells upon a slender stalk,
Lilies of the valley deck my garden walk,
Oh don't you wish that you could hear them ring?
That will happen only when the fairies sing.

That little song sent her creeping up the lily of the valley plants with their small white bells. "Surely," she thought, "I will hear them ring one day."

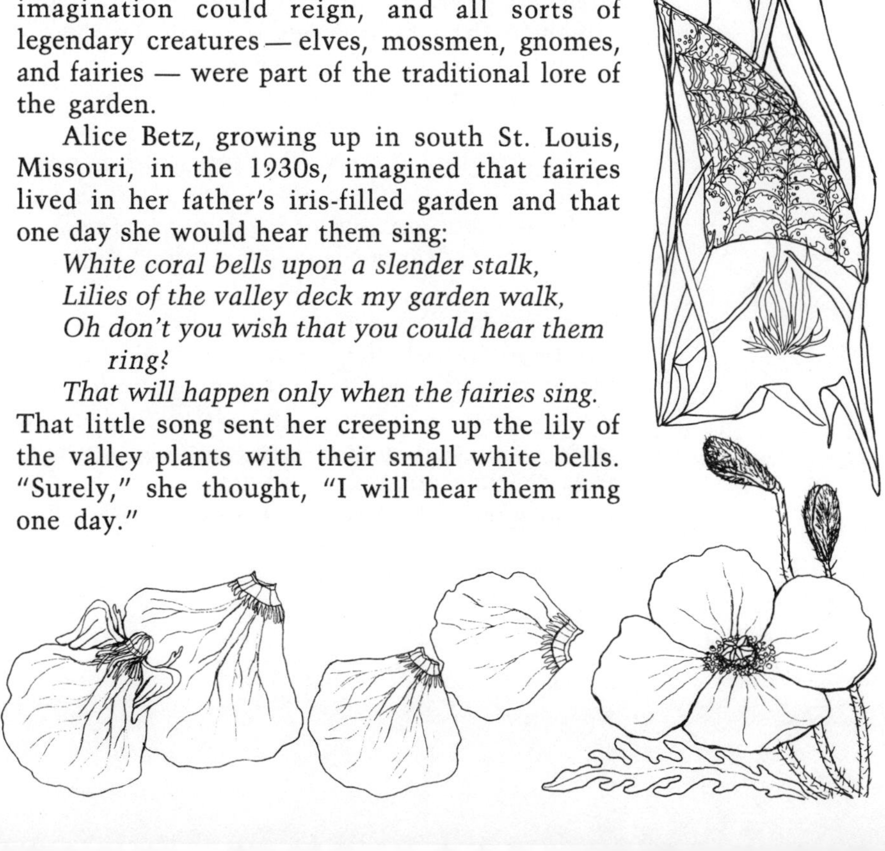

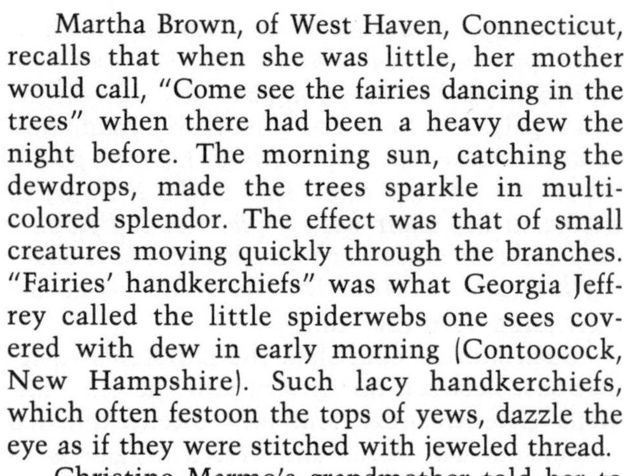

Martha Brown, of West Haven, Connecticut, recalls that when she was little, her mother would call, "Come see the fairies dancing in the trees" when there had been a heavy dew the night before. The morning sun, catching the dewdrops, made the trees sparkle in multicolored splendor. The effect was that of small creatures moving quickly through the branches. "Fairies' handkerchiefs" was what Georgia Jeffrey called the little spiderwebs one sees covered with dew in early morning (Contoocock, New Hampshire). Such lacy handkerchiefs, which often festoon the tops of yews, dazzle the eye as if they were stitched with jeweled thread.

Christine Marmo's grandmother told her to plant poppy seeds for the garden fairies and explained that the soft petals would be shawls for the tiny visitors. Alice Morse Earle also refers to this bit of lore in her book *Old Time Gardens*:

Each crumpled crepe-like leaf is soft as silk;
Long, long ago the children saw them there,
Scarlet and rose, with fringes white as milk
And called them "shawls for fairies' dainty wear"...

When they were nine, Lorraine Lauzon and her friend read all the books they could find on fairies and elves with the intent of building a "faerie garden"[9] where the little folk could dance on moonlit nights. After completing their research they created a one-yard-square garden patchworked with pieces of various mosses. The

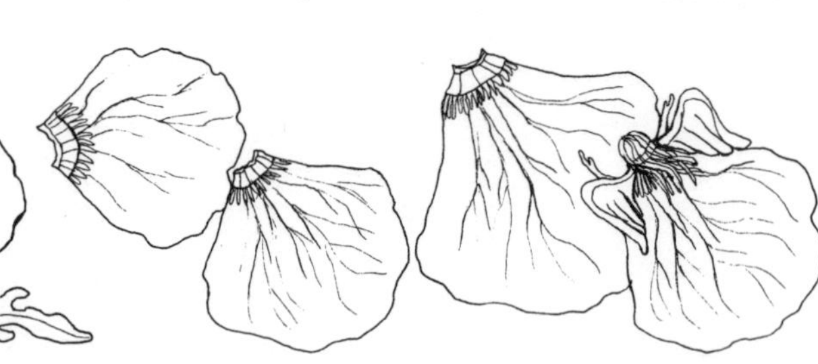

ring of mushrooms (to dance around) would not grow, so they set white beach pebbles in a circle. A water-filled saucer was a pool to reflect moonlight to attract the small creatures. When one morning a sparrow came to drink from the saucer, the girls knew that the garden was a success. (It is well known that during the daytime fairies often transform themselves into butterflies, insects, or birds.)

According to the ancients who named the flower and to children who are amused by it, each columbine is a circle of five doves or pigeons, heads inclined toward the center, tail feathers down. Another folk name, meeting-house flower, conjures up the image of a circle of the devout, heads bent in prayer.

Several plants had leaves that looked like small umbrellas to Alice Morse Earle and her friends:

*"The umbrellas are out!" call country children in spring when the leaves of May apple [*Podophyllum peltatum*] spread their umbrella-shaped lobes, and the little girls gather them and the leaves of the wild sarsaparilla [*Aralia nudicaulis*] for dolls' parasols. The spreading head of what we call snake grass [?] could also be tied into a very effective parasol.*

Mertensia virginica (Virginia bluebells, lungwort, Virginia cowslip) has flowers shaped like a child's straight-waisted, full-skirted frock,

and a calyx like a tiny green hat. Little girls made dolls out of these little flowers by first sticking pins upright in a piece of wood, then hanging the blossoms over them. The little pink and blue ladies seemed to dance in every passing breeze.

This dollmaking had an unforseen consequence on a Sunday afternoon in the 1850s in Worcester, Massachusetts. Since Puritan days, the New England Sabbath was to be spent quietly. After church, adults remained indoors reading, napping, or conversing in lowered voices. Children, if allowed outdoors, were to find clean and quiet pastimes in keeping with the sanctity of the day. Playing with dolls or other toys was forbidden, but gathering flowers was sometimes deemed appropriate. On this particular Sunday in spring, a little girl was allowed to pick mertensia and to use some of the pins from her sewing box. She made some little dolls, "carefully arranged her ladies in quadrilles and was very cheerfully playing dancing party to beguile the hours of that weary Sunday afternoon." The girl's horrified mother put an end to the game. No one, not even a doll, was allowed to dance on a Sunday![10]

Ever since the 1840s, when bleeding heart (native to China) was introduced to England, it has been a favorite garden flower. Children are drawn to it, as Alice Morse Earle writes:

The bleeding heart is a flower of inexpli-

cable charm to children: it has something of that mystery which in human nature we term fascination. Little children beg to pick it, and babies stretch out their tiny hand to it when showier blossoms are unheeded.

Part of its appeal is surely the shape of the flower, which has given rise to several folk names — lady's eardrop, lady's locket, and the most common, bleeding heart. Other common names are based on the inner construction of the flower. When the pink outer layer is pulled down on each side, the result looks like someone in a gondola, hence "lady-in-a-boat"! For those who think that the gondola looks more like a bathtub, "lady-in-a-bath" is another name. Swedish children call the flower lieutenant's heart. Kerstin Thunmark of Stockholm explains why: *"If you turn one small flower upside down and carefully pull aside the two pink-coloured pieces . . . you will see what is on the soldier's mind — a dancing girl and a bottle!"*

If the pink parts are removed altogether, a lyre or Irish harp can be seen within a heart-shaped frame. The lyre can be dissected out, leaving only the frame, as Alice Morse Earle recalls: *"Many scores have I carefully dissected, trying to preserve intact in skeleton shape the little heart frame of the delicate flower."*

Bernice Gildart (Northville, Michigan, early 1920s) remembers finding a baseball bat and a slipper in her dissections. Cheryl Dorschner (Wisconsin) also found (ballet) slippers; in addi-

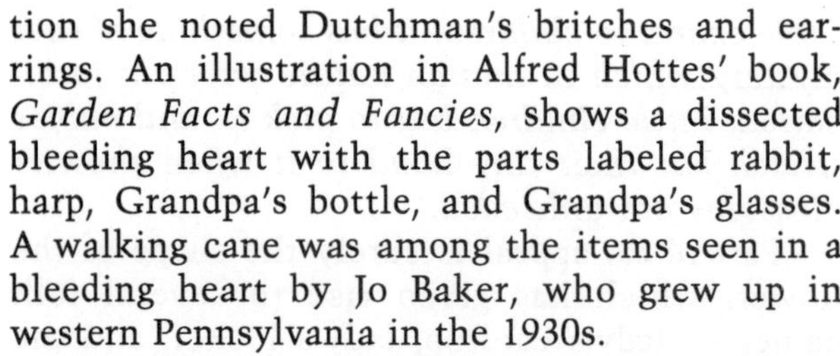

tion she noted Dutchman's britches and earrings. An illustration in Alfred Hottes' book, *Garden Facts and Fancies*, shows a dissected bleeding heart with the parts labeled rabbit, harp, Grandpa's bottle, and Grandpa's glasses. A walking cane was among the items seen in a bleeding heart by Jo Baker, who grew up in western Pennsylvania in the 1930s.

In 1918 an elderly gentleman, a family friend, showed Hilda Badger Drummond how to make a captivating little coach with bunny horses out of several bleeding heart flowers. The coach was one whole large bloom set on its side; the white protruding part was a harness or traces for the horses. Each bunny was one-half of the outer portion of the flower, taken off carefully and arranged ahead of the coach. To three-year-old Hilda, this creation looked like a miniature version of Cinderella's coach.

In addition to being imaginative, children from two to six are tireless seekers of knowledge. While trying to make sense out of the world, they may think that plants and even nonliving things are able to move at will, to think, or to talk. (For example, they may think that trees can decide to make the wind blow by moving their branches vigorously.) And children everywhere think for a time that nonliving objects can grow or regenerate. When he was three, Alan Turing, the brilliant British mathematician, buried a set of toy sailors in hopes of growing a set

of brand-new ones. Kornei Chukovsky, author of *From Two to Five*, noticed Russian children who did similar things:

Liosha buried a meat bone under his window and watered the spot regularly to grow a cow. Every morning he ran out to see if the cow's horns had sprouted yet.

In a diary that he kept about his 3½-year-old daughter, Chukovsky wrote this poem:

Mura took off her slipper,
Planted it in the garden —
"Grow, grow my little slipper,
I'll water you every day,
And a tree will grow.
A miracle tree!"
Barefooted children
To the miracle tree
Will hop and skip,
Pretty red booties
They will pick,
Saying:
"Oh, you, Murochka,
Oh, you clever one!"

Mary Anderson, who grew up in Ohio, remembers the following incident, which took place in 1926 when she was the same age as the slipper-planting Mura.

My first remembrance of gardening was [of] my parents making a hole with a stick and dropping in onion sets. My sister and I watched with great interest.

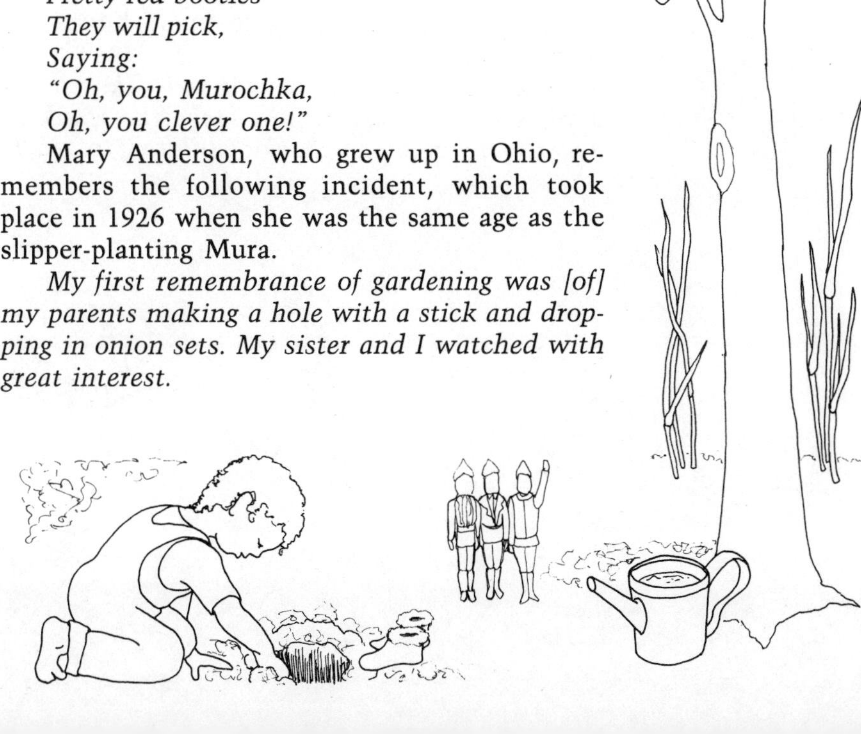

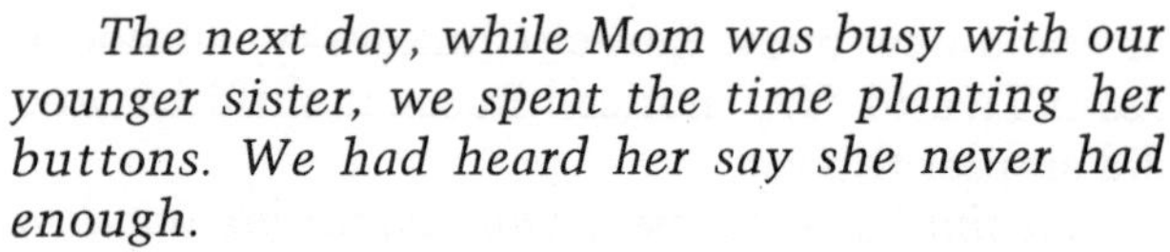

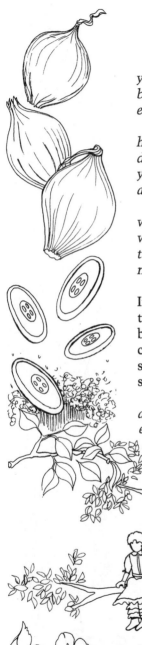

The next day, while Mom was busy with our younger sister, we spent the time planting her buttons. We had heard her say she never had enough.

Finally after so many trips in and out of the house, she asked, "Just what are you two girls doing?" My older sister said, "Mommy, next year you'll have all the buttons you need. Mary and I just planted all of yours."

Mom "planted" several well-deserved whacks and sent us out to dig the buttons up — which wasn't as easy as it sounds. I heard her tell many people she never accumulated as many buttons as her first button box held.

In Alice Morse Earle's garden in the late 1850s there grew handsomely gnarled apple trees that bore no fruit except a group of little girls. She called them "playhouse apple trees" because she and her friends spent so many hours ensconced atop them.

There is no play space for girls like an old apple tree. The main limbs leave the trunk at exactly the right height for children to reach,

and every branch and twig seems to grow and turn only to form delightful perches for children to climb among and cling onto. Some apple trees in our town had a copy of an Elizabethan garden furnishing; their branches enclosed tree platforms about twelve feet from the ground, reached by a narrow ladder or stairs. These were built by generous parents for their children's playhouses but their approach of ladder was too unhazardous, their railings too safety-assuring to prove anything but conventional and uninteresting. The natural apple tree offered infinite variety and a slight sense of daring to the climber.

Down on the ground, children also chose their own favorite places to play house. A "cubby" under two sheltering bushes was often preferred over a formal playhouse. Stones and stumps were set up for tables and chairs; forsythia blooms were golden lanterns for the playhouse. The inhabitants of the house went about in dandelion-stem curls and quince-petal nail polish. They seated their dolls under May-apple leaf parasols and entertained them at tea parties.

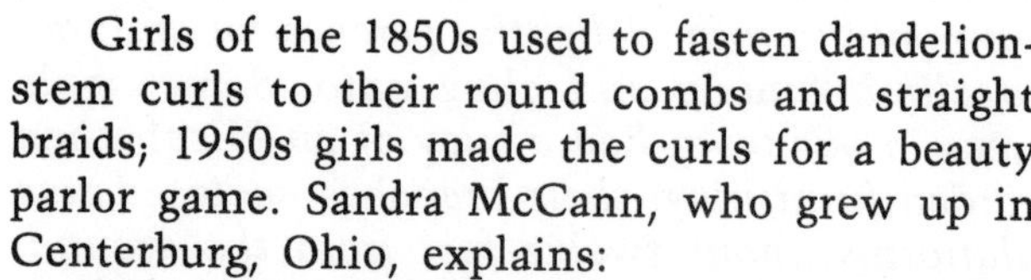

Girls of the 1850s used to fasten dandelion-stem curls to their round combs and straight braids; 1950s girls made the curls for a beauty parlor game. Sandra McCann, who grew up in Centerburg, Ohio, explains:

My cousin, Barbara Hankins Thatcher, introduced us to the game of beauty parlor, which required a container of water and several long-stemmed dandelions. We made several slits in one end of each stem and dunked the split end into the water to watch the permanent take place. A quick dip gave a body perm with loose curls; a longer dip produced tight curls. After we each had a perm, we imagined where we gorgeously coiffed ladies would go.

Getting the dandelions led to trouble for another 1950s child, Jane Lynch of Ashville, Ohio:

Once I borrowed my mother's butcher knife, which I was not permitted to have. After cutting the dandelions, I was pitching the knife and sticking it in the ground. I stuck it in the top of my foot and had to have stitches. (I told my parents a snake bit me!)

In the late spring when the days were long and lazy, more like summer than spring, the flowers of *Calycanthus florida* filled the garden air with a haunting scent. Its common names sing of the perfume of this flower: sweet shrub, strawberry shrub, and Carolina allspice. A favorite way to enjoy sweet shrub was to crush a flower or two in a handkerchief and carry it about. The scent, remembered so well even years later, was not easy for Alice Morse Earle to describe:

They have an aromatic fragrance somewhat like the ripest pineapple . . . but still richer; how I love to carry them in my hand, crushed and warm, occasionally holding them tightly over my mouth and nose to fill myself with their perfume. The leaves have a similar but somewhat varied and sharper scent, and woody stems another; the latter I like to nibble.

The scents of childhood are held fast in memory, often linked to entire scenes. The adult Proust, upon encountering again the scent of lime-flower tea, was transported back to his childhood village, Combray. To Louise Beebe Wilder, the scent of sweet shrub was the key to a "gate long closed upon a joyous childhood." She wrote in 1938:

One sniff of the spicy exhilarating odor and open flies the gate . . . and with the brown talisman held within my palm I am free to pass through a land of perpetual revels, where all wonders are possible and where faith in life . . . is as firm as the walls which guard the garden.

In Xenia, Ohio, June brought the scent of yellow sweet clover drifting over the town from

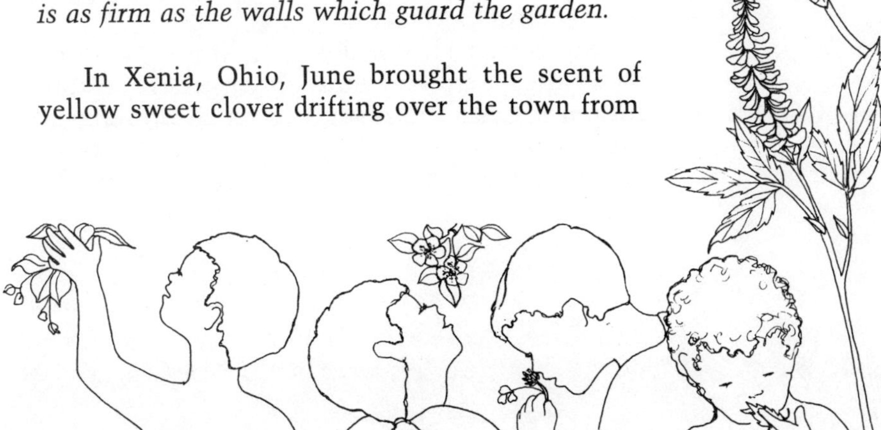

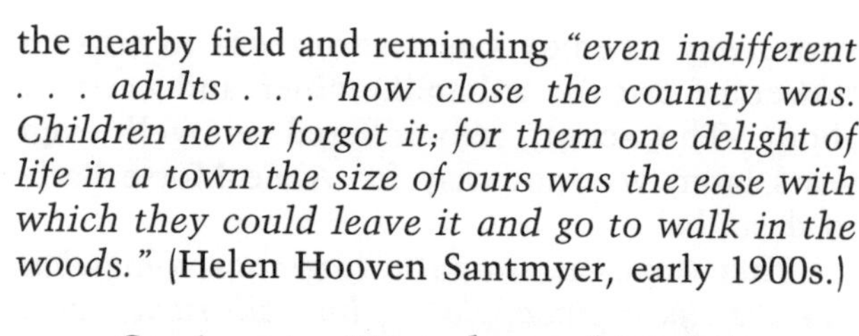

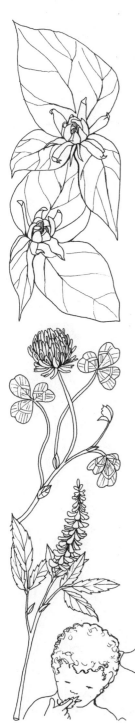

the nearby field and reminding *"even indifferent . . . adults . . . how close the country was. Children never forgot it; for them one delight of life in a town the size of ours was the ease with which they could leave it and go to walk in the woods."* (Helen Hooven Santmyer, early 1900s.)

Spring in Woods and Fields

As children roamed the woods and fields they nibbled, sniffed, peered at, and touched plants to discover their characteristics. In spring the tender new growth of many plants provided sweet or tangy treats. Children learned what plants to eat and what to avoid from older children who were eager to show off what they knew and to tell younger ones what not to do. As children grew old enough to walk into the woods and fields, each absorbed the traditional folklore accumulated over the centuries. Recalling the 1860s, Alice Morse Earle writes:

*The children ate an astonishing range: roots, twigs, leaves, bark, tendrils, fruit, berries, flowers, buds, seeds, all alike served for food. Young shoots of sweetbrier and blackberry are nibbled as well as the branches of young birch. Grapevine tendrils have an acid zest as do sorrel [*Rumex acetosella*] leaves.*

Sweetbrier shoots (*Rosa eglanteria*) were so sweet they were known as "brier candy." Biting into new twigs of sassafras left a clean, refreshing sensation in the mouth. The leaf buds of spruce and linden were other treats of spring. In

New England and Canada, country children gathered and ate the young fronds of cinnamon fern.[11] These furry green fiddleheads have a crisp white interior with a nutlike flavor. The bitter aftertaste did not deter the young foragers who eagerly sought out these buckhorns.

The tangy taste of cat brier (*Smilax rotundifolia*) attracted children, who called this treat "bread and butter."[12] In England, children nibble the leaves of the hawthorn tree and call this snack "bread and cheese."

The inner bark (cambium) of the white pine (*Pinus strobus*) is juicy; gathered in small strips, it was a woodsy dessert.[13]

Boys rambling through the woods of early spring might break off a few winter buds of alder to chew. Along their route they would leave behind spatterings of olive-green spittle in the lingering snow.[14]

Wintergreen (*Gaultheria procumbens*) berries that had wintered over after ripening in the fall, were larger and juicier in early spring.[15] Tender new leaves of this plant (also called teaberry, checkerberry, checkermint, and ivryleaves) were red, with the same aromatic flavor associated with wintergreen candies and gum.

Children called the ugly galls on oak leaves "oak apples" and sucked the sweet juice out of them.[16] (These growths, an inch to an inch and a half in diameter, are produced by gall-wasps on the new leaves of red, black, and scarlet oaks).

Fleshy gall-like swellings sometimes appear

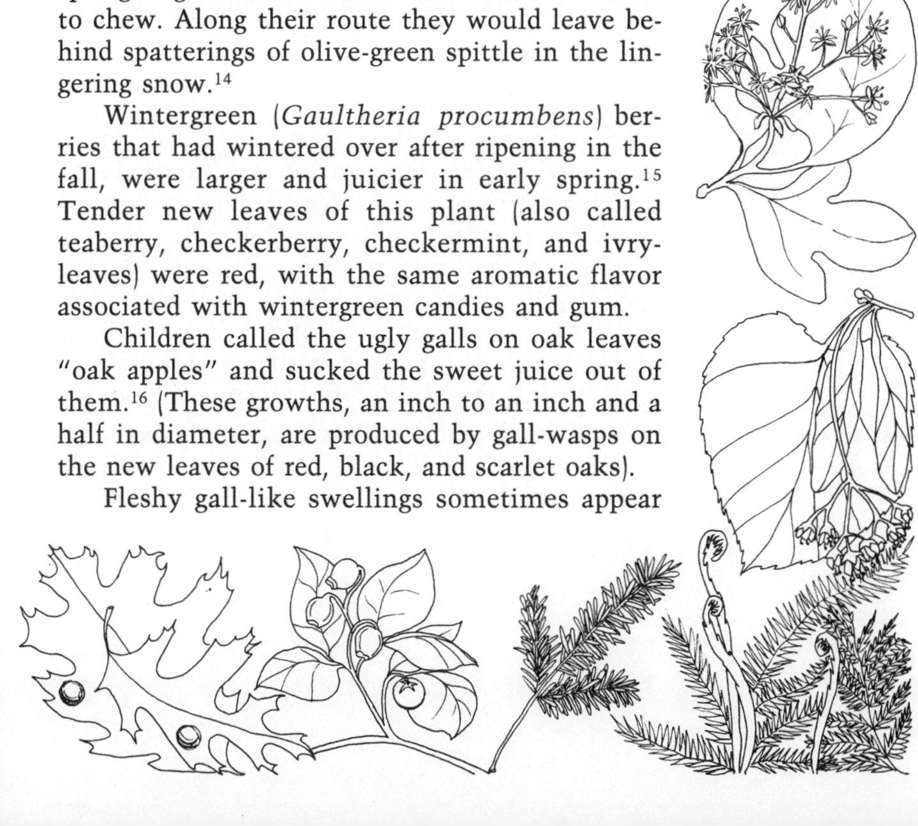

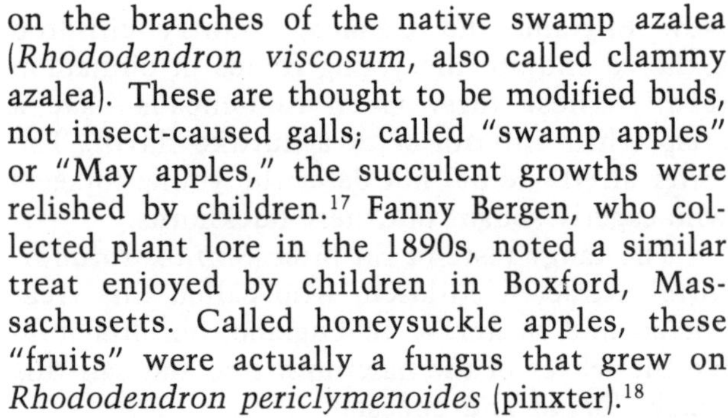

on the branches of the native swamp azalea (*Rhododendron viscosum*, also called clammy azalea). These are thought to be modified buds, not insect-caused galls; called "swamp apples" or "May apples," the succulent growths were relished by children.[17] Fanny Bergen, who collected plant lore in the 1890s, noted a similar treat enjoyed by children in Boxford, Massachusetts. Called honeysuckle apples, these "fruits" were actually a fungus that grew on *Rhododendron periclymenoides* (pinxter).[18]

Nibbling on plants while out on long spring walks was much more fun than being dosed at home with "spring tonics." Sassafras root tea, a tonic that Lila Ritter remembers with distaste from rural Kentucky in the 1920s, was thought to purify the blood. According to Bergen (1899), boys and girls went out to dig sassafras roots for tea in early spring and often would leave a bundle of roots for an elderly or sick neighbor.[19]

Equally as appealing as the tastes of spring were the visual experiences as hundreds of wildflowers appeared — food for color-starved eyes. They were greeted enthusiastically, as friends who had returned after a long absence. Purple, yellow, and white violets, white and pink trilliums, lady's slippers, wild sweet william, dogtooth violets, spring beauties, and bloodroot were among the children's favorites. Bloodroot they picked just to see the red "blood" drip out of the stem even though they knew the white flower would wilt before they got it home. The white trilliums looked like stars scattered on a background of brown fallen leaves; they stayed in bloom for weeks and became first pale pink then deep rose in a magical transformation. The tiny yellow dogtooth violets (*Erythronium americanum*) had leaves appealingly spotted with brown.

Some plants, named for articles of clothing, were scrutinized to see if they really resembled lady's slippers or Dutchman's breeches. Marsh marigolds were pure gold; their color looked more intense by being set against a background of dark, oozy mud. But was it worth the somewhat scary walk through the swamp to find them? Jumping from tussock to tussock, the children reminded each other about "cows that had sunk in the mud up to their horns." Looking fearfully

around, they almost expected to see horns sticking up to verify the rumor.

Everyone had a favorite walk, taken so often that the terrain and plants became second nature. J. Stewart remembers these effortless lessons:

Without benefit of a wildflower book I learned which flowers grew in wet, and which in dry; what plants would only be in a sunny place and what grew in shady nooks; those that I would find by rocks, and those that would be in the open in the company of grass. I knew the order of bloom — which flowers came first in the spring and then next and next after that . . . I knew how the stems felt in my hand — soft or brittle and which exuded a sap. As for the flowers, I knew which would wilt, which could be

gathered for bouquets, and which should be left because they were scarce.

Knowledge not so easily come by was the appearance of the plants in late summer or fall. Since spring was so wondrous and the woods so easy to walk in, I went exploring every day and looked carefully. But summer was a time to do other things, and the woods became brambly. When time came to walk in the woods later in the season I would find plants with white berries, or with bunches of glossy red berries, or sprays of blue berries. Which of these went with the flowers seen in spring? This was lore that was not passed along to me; I later looked in wildflower guides to find out.

One rule that every country child knew was: don't put any plant into your mouth until you

have been shown by an older child or adult that it is safe to eat. And we found out that some plants had only certain parts that were edible. One friend had a grandmother who played a leaf-matching game with us kids. She would pick five edible leaves, then hold one up and say, "Match this leaf." We had to go find a plant with a matching leaf. Soon we knew which salad greens to pick.

Violets carpeted the woods on many a child's favorite walk. The breathtaking sight of the violets blooming *en masse* excited the children, who fell upon the flowers, gathering them by the handfuls. Could washing in the dew of violets prevent freckles? Sandra Bayes and her friends in Urbana, Ohio, tried this in the 1940s on their faces and shoulders. "Although every-

one swore this would work, nothing happened," recalls Bayes. Wearing leaf hats trimmed with violets (with a sprig of fern for a feather), a couple of Alabama girls imitated their favorite movie stars:

Emily was radiant as Norma Talmadge, while I was a seductive Bebe Daniels. We invented the story as we went along, describing our dresses and sweethearts to a spellbound audience of cows. (Evelyn Vincent, 1930s.)

Late in the afternoon of April 30, children went to gather flowers for May baskets. May Day[20] or May Basket Day (May 1) was Kay Kaufmann's favorite holiday. Growing up in central Iowa in the late 1930s and early 1940s (the war years), she recalls how she and her friends celebrated May Day:

We would roll paper into cone shapes or fold a square piece of paper into a basket shape and glue on a paper handle. Sometimes, if we were lucky, we had colored paper and lacy paper doilies to use. We would pick the beautiful woods flowers and fill the baskets. (If there were not enough wildflowers we would pick some yard flowers like lilacs, sweet peas, and pansies.) Then we would add popcorn and homemade cookies. We would take the baskets around our neighborhood to the homes of friends and elderly neighbors. After hanging a basket on someone's doorknob, we would run and hide, hoping to see the person open the door and find the basket.

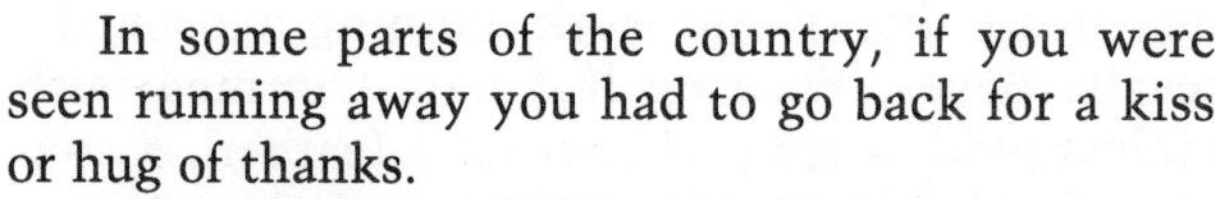

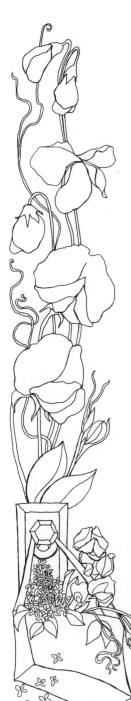

In some parts of the country, if you were seen running away you had to go back for a kiss or hug of thanks.

When William Wells Newell was growing up in Massachusetts (1820s), the young men went out in search of flowers in the chilly dawn of May 1. Each made a "basket" out of greens (wintergreen leaves, princess pine, etc.) and *"cautiously affixed it to the door of any girl he wished to honor. She was left to guess the giver."* The young women had their own customs, as Newell remembers:

In those days, troops of young girls might still be seen, bareheaded and dressed in white, their May-queen crowned with a garland of paper.

Violets were not just for bouquets; children since the 1700s had demolished violets in contests known as violet wars, fighting roosters, or fighting cocks. This game, originally played in England, was popular with American children of the nineteenth century and is still played today. Two players each start with an equal number of violets. Each takes one violet in hand and hooks the head of his flower under the head of his opponent's violet. Alice Morse Earle explains that *"the projecting spur under the curved stem at the base of the violet was a hook, and when the flowers clinched, we pulled until the stronger was conqueror and the weaker head was off."* The winner of each round got to keep the loser's flower head. Whoever accumulated the most heads won the game.[21]

Another flower-beheading contest was done with dandelions. Flicking off the top from the stem with their thumb, contestants would see whose flower would shoot the farthest. They accompanied the flicking action with a singsong rhyme: *"A lady had a baby, and its head popped off!"* (1960s, Carol DeFeciani, Haverstraw, New York.)

The buckhorn (ribwort plantain, *Plantago lanceolata*) flower heads were also used as projectiles in a "rambunctious game with brothers," remembers Starr Howington from her rural New Jersey childhood during the 1950s. With Algerian ivy leaves as shields against the assault of plaintain guns, David Johnson and his friends battled in an abandoned lot in Berkeley, California, in the 1950s. Some kids, such as Anne Benko of Sayerville, New Jersey, would "make a bend in the stem and slip the top part of the plant through this bend." She adds that, "By pulling on the stem behind the head, we would shoot one another." David Johnson comments, "If the inflorescence is just ripe enough, a slight tug sends it ahead about four or five feet." Another way of shooting was to bend the stem of a second plantain into an inverted V, and pull the flower head sharply through the point of the V.

Other combats enlivened the spring days. Sherwood Moran, who spent his days as a missionary kid in Japan, remembers making swords of bamboo grass:

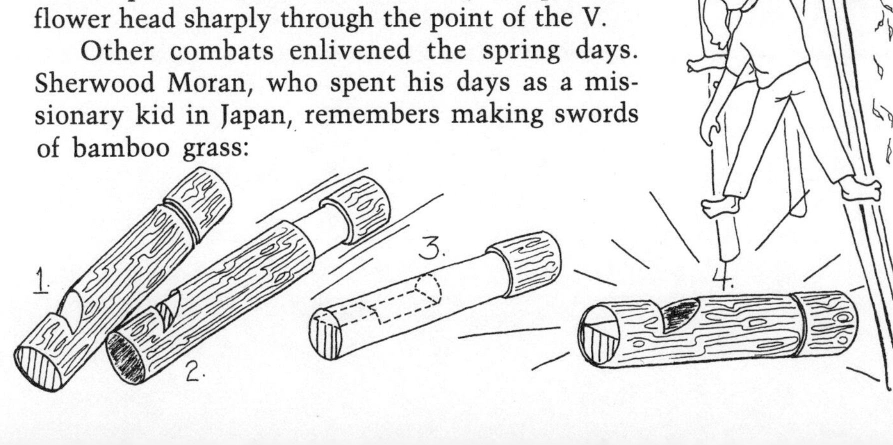

We would break off the long leaves, form a shaft of the center spine, and bend the left and right sides of the blade of grass around the middle finger of the left hand, letting the center spine protrude toward our enemy. By rapidly pulling the two sides downward with your right hand, forcing the slender spine forward, we had a fairly harmless weapon. We would often hold contests for distance.

Last year's cattails, now brittle and brown, made spears and javelins for vigorous battles.

When the dogwood bloomed, it was time to make willow and hickory whistles. Alice Morse Earle (1860s) lists the making of an "ear-piercing" willow whistle among boys' accomplishments. In 1918 Hilda Badger Drummond's father took her on a walk to a place in Newton Highlands, Massachusetts, called Bacon Farm. She recalls: *"There, at the edge of a marsh, he cut just the right piece of willow branch and before my very eyes he created a lovely whistle for me."*

Effie Russell, of Kentucky, made her 1930s whistles out of hickory:

In the spring when the sap begins to rise, cut a small branch from a hickory tree (about four or five inches long and one inch in diameter). Cut the bark in the center, then turn or tap lightly to loosen one end of the bark. It should slip off easily because of the sap. Cut a small groove or slanted place in the top of the wood; make a

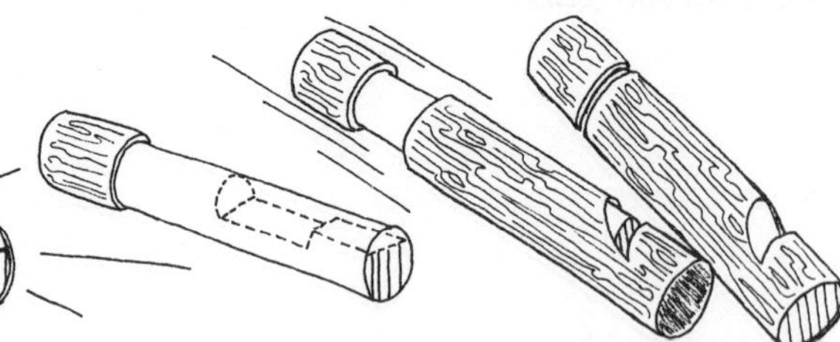

hole in the bark at the same place. There is the magic whistle!

Some kids used other kinds of wood to make these simple instruments as well as more intricate slide-bark whistles.[22]

Exploring the terrain near home, children often came upon plants that, according to their older friends, could bring good luck, answer questions, or grant wishes. Dandelions and buttercups were the two flowers most commonly associated with such superstitions. Dandelions appeared first, dotting the roadsides with bright yellow and delighting the children. They asked one another, "Do you like butter?" and held dandelions under each other's chins to look for the yellow glow that indicates "yes." The later-blooming buttercup was the flower most associated with this little ritual. According to Claire Shaver Haughton, the author of *Green Immigrants*, the question originally asked of buttercups in medieval rituals was, "Will I be rich?" with the answering yellow reflection to affirm. Buttercups are linked with gold in several legends, such as the following:

(Have you ever heard that at the end of every rainbow there is a pot of gold? Well, here is a story about a little boy who went looking for that gold.)

Once upon a time there was a little boy who decided to find the pot of gold at the end of the rainbow. Many other people had looked for this

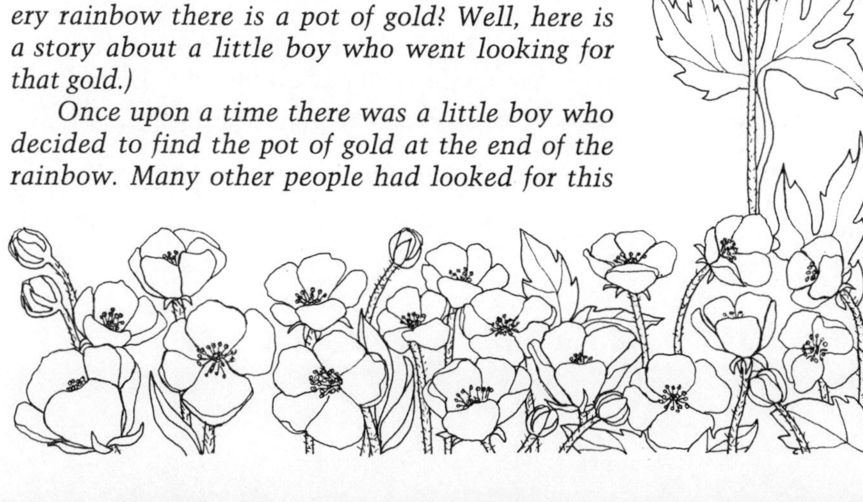

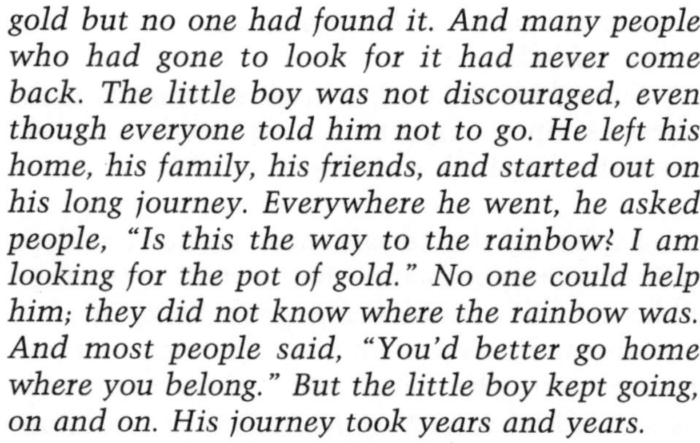

gold but no one had found it. And many people who had gone to look for it had never come back. The little boy was not discouraged, even though everyone told him not to go. He left his home, his family, his friends, and started out on his long journey. Everywhere he went, he asked people, "Is this the way to the rainbow? I am looking for the pot of gold." No one could help him; they did not know where the rainbow was. And most people said, "You'd better go home where you belong." But the little boy kept going, on and on. His journey took years and years.

One night after he had lain down to go to sleep, a beautiful lady in shimmering white robes appeared. She held up a mirror and when the little boy looked in, what do you think he saw? He was looking at his own face but did not recognize it because it was the face of an old man — wrinkled and tired-looking. His journey had taken him so many years that he had grown old looking for the gold.

The old man cried out, "I'm so old now, I'll never find the gold." But the shining lady looked at him and very sadly said, "You will find the gold, but it will not make you happy! You have spent your whole life looking for that money and have never helped anyone else. Other people have been in trouble and have needed you, but you were too busy to pay attention to them."

The lady disappeared and the old man fell asleep.

When he got up the next morning, the man

was up on a high hill looking down into a deep valley. A light rain was falling with the sun shining through the raindrops, making a bright colored rainbow which touched down in the valley right below where the old man was standing. He stumbled down the hillside and found the treasure he had been looking for all his life. (The gold was not in a pot as everyone had always said; it was in a brown cloth bag.) The old man did not want anyone to steal his bag of gold, so he decided to dig a hole and bury it. He waited all day until it was dark so that no one would see him. He walked along a brook and through a meadow looking for a good place to bury the gold.

As he walked, an elf came up behind him and cut a small hole in the bag. The gold coins began to fall out, one by one, onto the grass. The old man never noticed that his bag was getting lighter and lighter. His path was marked by the sparkling pieces of gold he had dropped. The elves decided to fasten stems to the gold coins so they would not sink down into the dirt. All night long the little folk worked. At sunrise the grass of the meadow was decorated with a path of beautiful gold flowers that wound along beside the brook. The old man was so upset when he found his money was gone that he disappeared. No one ever saw him again, but every year the golden flowers come up to mark his path.[23]

Kim Standard, a "fifth generation Atlantan,"

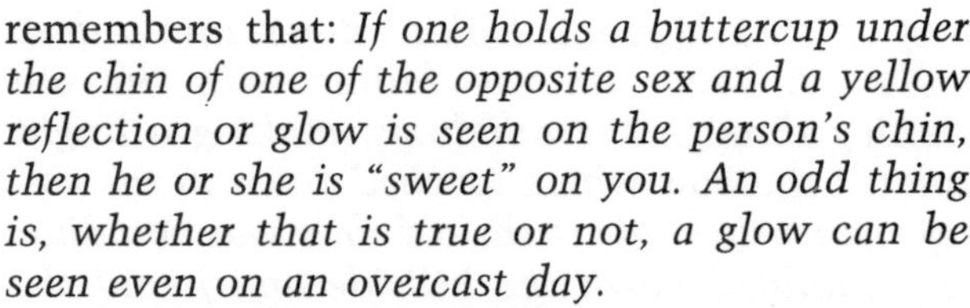

remembers that: *If one holds a buttercup under the chin of one of the opposite sex and a yellow reflection or glow is seen on the person's chin, then he or she is "sweet" on you. An odd thing is, whether that is true or not, a glow can be seen even on an overcast day.*

Pat Talbert and her friends in Oakland, California, held dandelions under each other's chins *"to see how much sweetness we contained. The brighter the yellow reflection, the sweeter you were."*

Dandelion seedheads had more customs connected with them than did any flower. Carried into the air by a child's quick puff of breath, these small seed "parachutes" could tell time, answer questions, and make wishes come true. Alice Morse Earle, recalling the 1850s, wrote:

When the dandelion had lost her golden locks and had grown old and gray, the children still plucked the downy heads, the "clocks" or "blowballs," and fortifying young lungs with a deep breath, they blew upon the head to see "whether mother wants me" or to learn the time of day.

To find out if mother wanted them, children blew on the seedhead three times. If all the seeds were gone, then mother didn't need them at home. If any seeds were left, it was time to head for home immediately! Geoffrey Charlesworth, who grew up in Yorkshire, England, in the 1920s, explains that *"dandelions were used to tell the time: you blew the clock until all the seeds had gone, counting at the same time."*[24]

If you took one puff, it was one o'clock. If it took three puffs to dislodge all the seeds, it was three o'clock, and so forth. If you had played hookey and were hiding until school was over, a dandelion could tell you when it was safe to come out. Since many rural schools let out at four, the truant looked for a seedhead that needed at least four puffs to empty it.

Dandelion, the globe of down,
The schoolboy's clock in every town,
which the truant puffs amain
To conjure back long hours again.[25]

Another way to tell time was to take one puff and count the remaining seeds. The number was the time of day.

A more romantic superstition linked with dandelion seeds was this: to find out if a certain boy or girl liked you, you blew on the seedhead. If after one puff no seeds were left, your sweetheart loved you and only you. If there were a few seeds left, he or she was interested in others, and if there were many seeds left, the loved one didn't even know you existed.

"How many children will I have?" was another question asked of the seedhead. The answer was the number of seeds left after one puff. If you didn't puff really vigorously, the answer might be eight or nine children, a result that brought forth gales of laughter.

J. Stewart remembers that the most common

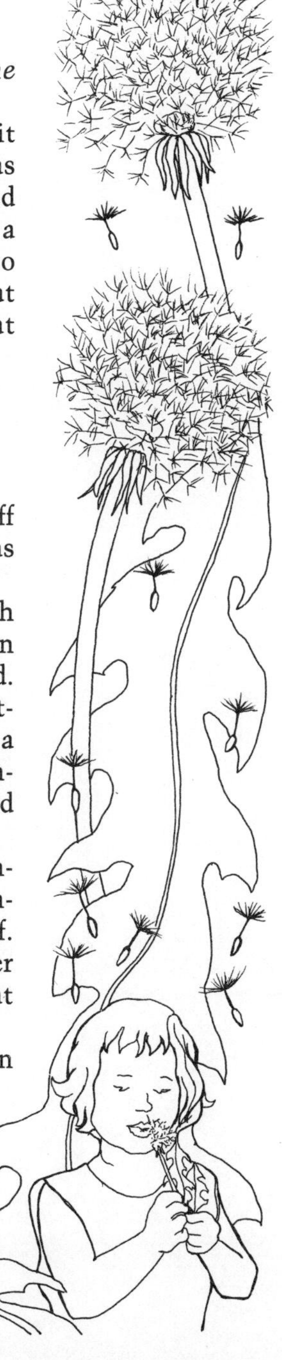

way of using dandelion seeds in western Massachusetts in the 1940s was to make wishes:

Just as we did with birthday candles, we would make a wish and then blow. If all the seeds were blown off with one puff, our wish would come true. Some kids counted the remaining seeds and said, "Your wish will come true in three or four (or however many seeds remained) days."

To Carol DeFeciani's great-grandmother, who called dandelions gone-to-seed "money blowers" (or money wishers), one strong puff promised wealth.

"In the 1930s we held parachute races with dandelion seedheads," recalls Virginia York. She and her friends in Delevan, Wisconsin, would "blow on the seedheads to see whose seeds would travel the farthest."

A source of great merriment to children was the idea that dandelions had something to do with wetting the bed. Norman Singer of Sandisfield, Massachusetts, comments: *"If you do not blow all the seeds off with one puff, you will pee the bed that night. Everyone knows that!"*

Geoffrey Charlesworth states that it is the *picking* of dandelion flowers that is unlucky, recalling that in Yorkshire dandelions were called "picklebeds" or "pissabeds." These common names were brought to America too, because Jeanné Smith (who grew up in Astoria, New York, in the 1920s) remarks, "All the kids called dandelions "pissabeds."[26]

Mustard, especially mustard seed, has long been considered lucky. J. Stewart remembers a mustard-seed necklace that many girls wore during the 1940s:

Suspended on a chain was a clear glass vial filled with water in which one mustard seed floated. I seem to recall that the necklaces came packaged on a card printed with a Bible verse, probably either Matthew XIII:31 ("The kingdom of heaven is like to a mustard seed") or Matthew XVII:20 ("If you have faith as a grain of mustard seed . . . nothing shall be impossible unto you").

Mustard (*Brassica* varieties) grew in early American kitchen gardens, then escaped to cover fields with sheets of gold. One of these fields of wild mustard was a cherished private place for Gloria Gerhold when she was a child:

I grew up in Pasadena, California, in the twenties, with open meadows filled with wildflowers. Next door, the meadow was a blaze of yellow every year — wonderful, fragrant mustard which every year grew about five feet tall. All the neighborhood children spent hours playing there — underneath — in long green tunnels we fashioned patiently, over an acre. It was such fun, as we could never be seen from the street or sidewalks.

Passersby might hear the voices of the children at play, but the maze of green tunnels was a hidden world, known only to its inhabitants.

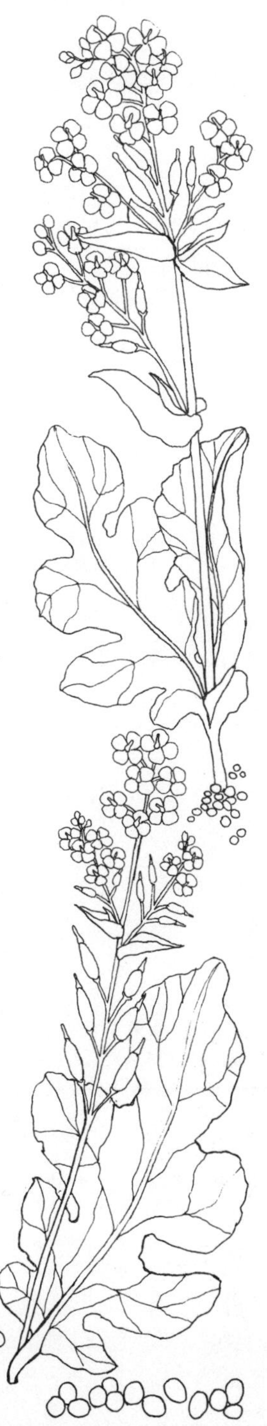

SUMMER IN THE GARDEN

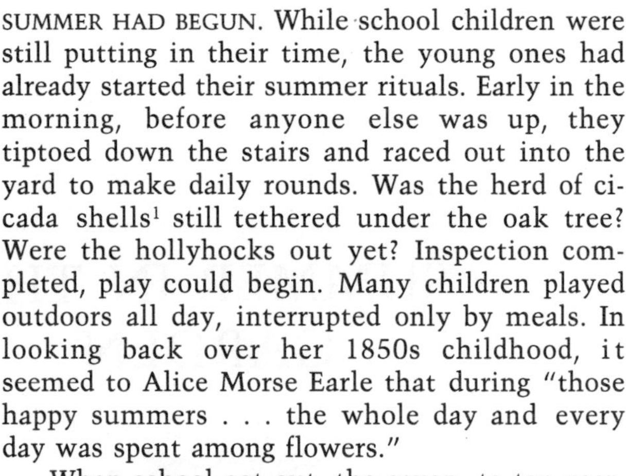

SUMMER HAD BEGUN. While school children were still putting in their time, the young ones had already started their summer rituals. Early in the morning, before anyone else was up, they tiptoed down the stairs and raced out into the yard to make daily rounds. Was the herd of cicada shells[1] still tethered under the oak tree? Were the hollyhocks out yet? Inspection completed, play could begin. Many children played outdoors all day, interrupted only by meals. In looking back over her 1850s childhood, it seemed to Alice Morse Earle that during "those happy summers . . . the whole day and every day was spent among flowers."

When school got out, the seven- to ten-year-olds joined in the life of the garden, leading small brothers, sisters, and friends in imaginative pastimes. Trees and bushes were their hideouts and playhouses. Flowers, leaves, and seeds of garden plants became props, costumes, jewelry, food for dolls, and noisemakers.

In summertime the old-fashioned garden was a paradise for a child . . . the long sunny days brought into life so many delightful playthings. . . .

Those old-fashioned gardens that Alice Morse Earle wrote about were filled with a wonderful mixture of flowers, fruits, and vegetables and often surrounded by a hedge or wooden fence.

The close juxtapositions and even interminglings of vegetables and fruit with the flowers

had a sense of homely simplicity and usefulness which did not detract from the garden's interest and added much to the child's pleasure.

One of Earle's favorite Worcester gardens was that of an elderly neighbor whom she and her mother often visited to exchange seeds, plants, and bulbs. In his flower borders were roses, peonies, and iris. Here, *"a close scent of box hung over the garden even in midwinter. . . . [A]t the lower end of this garden was a small orchard of the best Playhouse Apple trees I ever climbed; some large trees bearing little globular early pears; and there were rows of bushes of Honey-blob gooseberries.*

In 1900 the gardens of Xenia, Ohio, had the same satisfying mixture of fruit, vegetables, and flowers. From up in her favorite apple tree, five-year-old Helen Hooven Santmyer could look down upon a sea of neighboring yards:

Every path from back door to barn was covered by a grape arbor and every yard had its fruit trees. In the center of any open space remaining our grandfathers had planted syringas and sweet shrub, snowball, Rose of Sharon, and Balm of Gilead.

At ground level it would have been impossible to see these gardens because each was surrounded by a high fence. In the enclosed gardens even small children could be left to play:

The garden solitudes were ours alone. Our elders stayed in the dark houses or sat fanning on the front porch. They never troubled them-

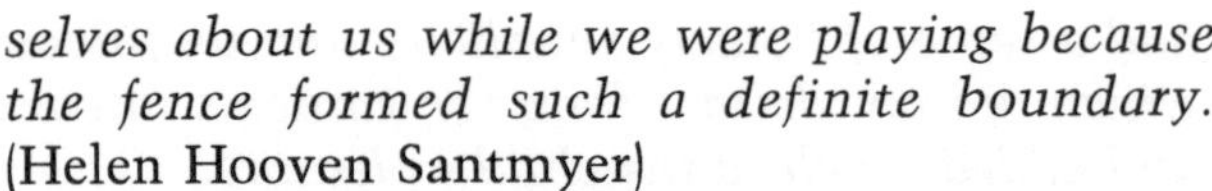

selves about us while we were playing because the fence formed such a definite boundary. (Helen Hooven Santmyer)

The fences made the children feel secure, "safe from interruption and possible amusement of the passersby." Helen and her friends wove the fences into their games of make-believe: a vine-covered wooden gatepost was Sleeping Beauty's enchanted castle, and Rapunzel let down her golden hair from the wrought iron heights of another post.

Hideouts

Each garden had its secret places where the children could hide and pretend to be on their own. Bean pole teepees and thicket wigwams in the vegetable garden became leafy hideaways, as did grape arbors, tall plants, and certain bushes.

Our favorite haunt, our dear Box House, was a very old bush of Buxus sempervirens, *perhaps a thicket of several, with five or six trunks densely branched from the ground, and just bare enough in its depths to provide us with a perfect hiding place. Its boughs, big and sturdy, were as many seats, tables and shelves. There we spent delightful moments, away from adult eyes, perhaps exchanging confidences. . . . (I realize now that we were like young ostriches — if grownups couldn't have seen us, they certainly heard us!)* (Rose-Marie Vassallo-Villaneau. Niort, France, 1950s.)

From Berkshire, County, Massachusetts, in the late 1930s, J. Stewart recalls:

My first hideout was a stand of ferns which grew alongside our cinder driveway. From inside the tall ferns I could see my whole yard and the dirt road where an occasional car or pedestrian went by. I reveled in the idea of being able to see out without being seen.

Billie Casey, who grew up in Texas in the 1920s, was the youngest child in her family by many years. Thus, as she says, "I was raised alone and had to entertain myself as best I could." Billie found a favorite spot in the back yard:

I would take my little celluloid dolls and hide out in the hollyhocks. I was small and they were big, as high as the house, and just beautiful. I would take my mother's dish towels and screen me off a place by myself and play for hours.

The close-growing trunks of lilac formed cubby-houses in Alice Morse Earle's garden. Spreading out "an old thick shawl . . . on the damp earth for a carpet." Alice and her friends spent hours in the lilac hideaway:

Oh, how hot and scant the air was in the green light of those "garden thickets," those "lilac ambushes" which were really not half so pleasant as the cooler seats under the trees, — but which we clung to with a warmth equal to their temperature. (1860s)

In the 1950s Phoebe Neigel and her three brothers hung out at Fig Tree Hotel. She reminisces about this hideout:

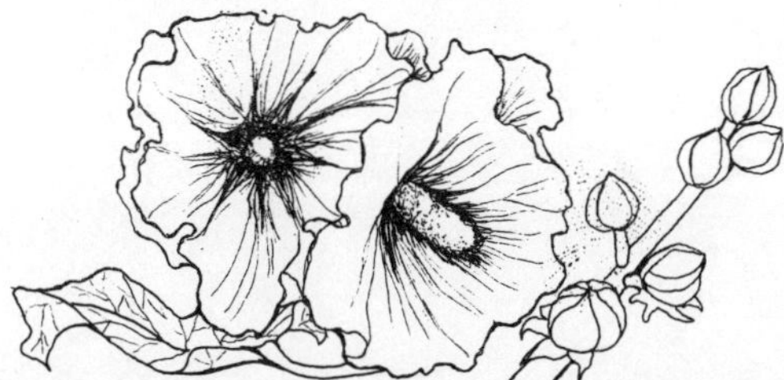

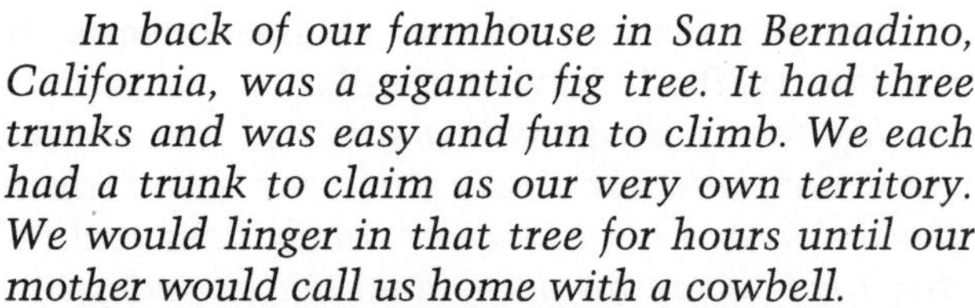

In back of our farmhouse in San Bernadino, California, was a gigantic fig tree. It had three trunks and was easy and fun to climb. We each had a trunk to claim as our very own territory. We would linger in that tree for hours until our mother would call us home with a cowbell.

Sometimes the children would eat lunch up in the tree and even invite their pet goats to join them.

We fashioned backpacks from empty burlap feed bags. I sewed lace and trim on mine and also poked wild flowers through the burlap. We put our baby kids in the bags, strapped them to our backs, and climbed into Fig Tree Hotel.

Playing House

In summer, as in spring, a favorite outdoor activity was playing house. Children cooked, cleaned, and entertained guests in various kinds of shelter. To LeAnne Arnold, any low, sweeping branch was a Green Mansion where she could set up housekeeping. Carol Holcomb, who grew up in the 1960s, found a similar spot in her back yard in Atlanta, Georgia:

The back forty feet of our lot, called The Woods, was densely planted with pines, maples, and dogwoods, never raked so the ground was all soft with pine needles and decomposed leaves. The pine trees formed an upper canopy; lower down were the dogwood trees whose wide spreading branches formed a low canopy over the ground. One of my favorite things to do was

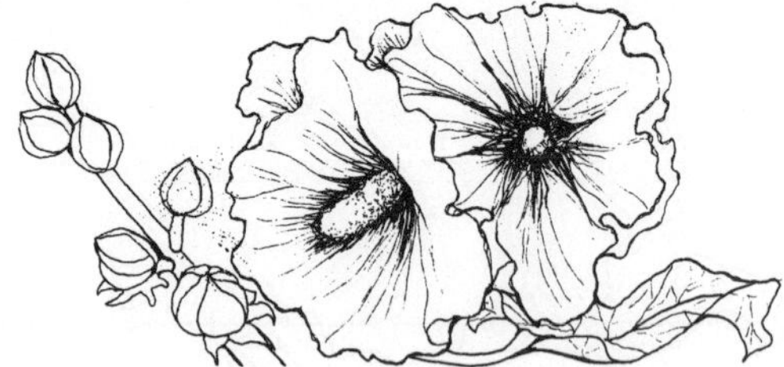

to creep underneath the leaf canopy and set up my little kitchen. I would construct a spit to cook on, and with a tiny scrap of lumber from my father's workshop I had a wonderful table. The spit and the table legs were made of twigs and I would search diligently to find two forked twigs so that my rotisserie would really turn. Sometimes I would find some red rose petals to put under the rotisserie for a real fire. If the twigs for the spit were slender enough, I would spear little leaves and cook them for a fine lunch.

Barbara Loftus and her brother played house and also café, a game in which she did the cooking:

I would mix mud, spread it on big poplar leaves, and fold them over — tacos! The tips of salt cedar branches in water made a super stew. Honeysuckle blossoms were always dessert. (We actually sipped those and also chewed sugar cane.) (El Paso, Texas, c. 1940.)

Having parties meant having to clean house, set the table, decorate the table, and prepare special foods. Of all the delicacies, mudpies led the list. J. Stewart declares:

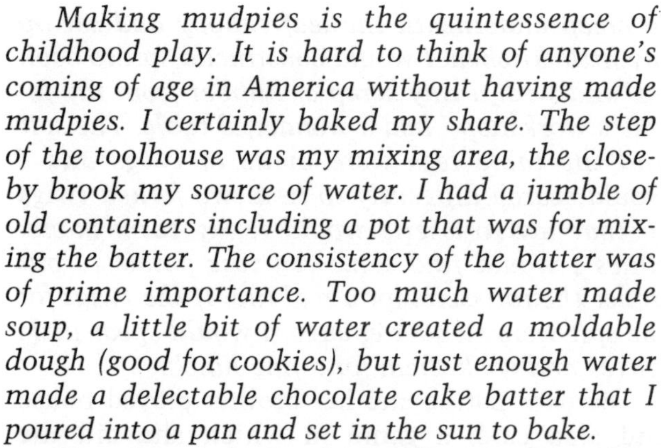

Making mudpies is the quintessence of childhood play. It is hard to think of anyone's coming of age in America without having made mudpies. I certainly baked my share. The step of the toolhouse was my mixing area, the close-by brook my source of water. I had a jumble of old containers including a pot that was for mixing the batter. The consistency of the batter was of prime importance. Too much water made soup, a little bit of water created a moldable dough (good for cookies), but just enough water made a delectable chocolate cake batter that I poured into a pan and set in the sun to bake.

Growing up in South Carolina in the 1960s, Barry Holcomb had a mudpie kitchen that his father made for him: *"I had a countertop of boards set up on bricks so that it could be taken down and stored from year to year."* Now his five-year-old son makes mudpies with the same native red clay, which, according to Barry's wife, Carol, *"makes excellent pies because it's as hard as rocks when it dries and wonderfully gooey when just the right amount of water is added."*

In Ohio during the twenties, Mary Anderson and her sister June spent many afternoons making mudpies. Their mother came out often to check on their play.

One day when Mother came out, June was missing, so Mother asked, "Mary, where did June go?" I answered, "Oh, she's in the hooken *house, getting* hooken *eggs." Well, Mother*

moved fast. We were properly punished and we got out of the mudpie-making business. We'd found out that, without eggs, our cakes and pies didn't have that stick-together consistency and didn't hold their shape.

For icing on her cakes Anne Benko used clay from the bottom of a nearby lake. Effie Russell lived near a "chalk gully" bottomed with multicolored soil; what a rainbow of frosting that made! Devona Elliott had a "bakery with all kinds of mud cakes, pies, and doughnuts, fancy decorated with my mother's flowers and imprinted with their leaves" (Wheeling, Indiana, 1930s). Colorful berries, the yellow centers of daisies, or seeds from grasses were the final fillip on the mud creations.

Most pretend foods were created from parts of plants that, in shape or color, resembled real foods. Lori Maple Hayes (1960s, Philadelphia, Pennsylvania) relates:

From the privet hedges that border many row homes we made collard greens, even taking the time to tear them (as mother does) while filling our pots and pans. In our travels we noted all spinach and string bean trees (weeping willow and catalpa).

From Beverly Elliott (California, 1930s): *The buttons [seed pods] of hollyhocks, peeled and sliced into wedges, made cheese served to dolls on their tiny dishes.*

Although Elliott used the seed cases only for

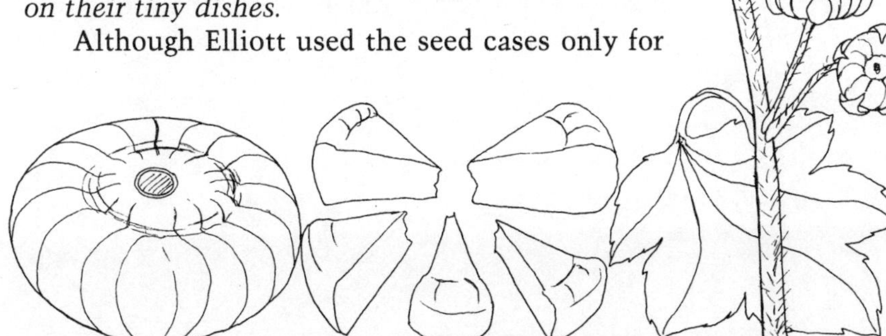

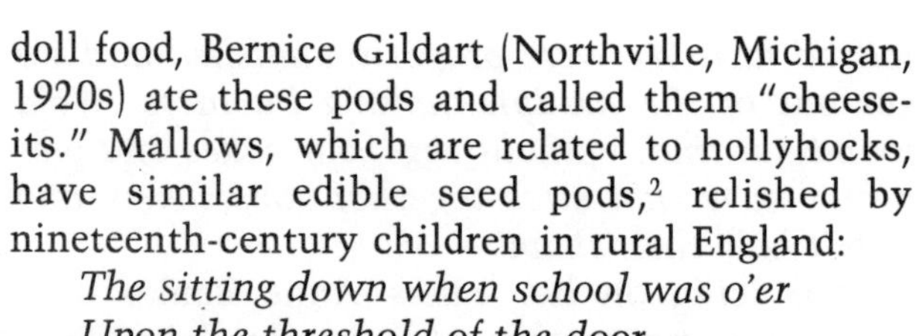

doll food, Bernice Gildart (Northville, Michigan, 1920s) ate these pods and called them "cheese-its." Mallows, which are related to hollyhocks, have similar edible seed pods,[2] relished by nineteenth-century children in rural England:

The sitting down when school was o'er
Upon the threshold of the door,
Picking from mallows, sport to please,
The crumpled seed we call a cheese.
(John Clare, 1793-1864)

Alice Morse Earle and her friends also ate these garden cheeses:

For the child's larder, hollyhocks furnished food in their mucilaginous cheeses . . . [and] a low growing mallow . . . wherever it chanced to run, shared with its cousin Hollyhock the duty of providing cheeses.

Cooking for dolls and pretend guests was done with whatever plant materials were readily available:

We cooked with the seeds from the numerous pine cones we gathered. If we had pine cones and maple seeds at the same time, we made casseroles. (Carol Holcomb)

I made concoctions with anything that would stain or make a mess. I stirred up "poisonous" brews of dandelion bloom, medicinal stews of maple seeds, grass seeds, bits of grass . . . and soups from any kind of interesting seed pods and leaf shreds. Hollyhock seeds got thrown into a soup. (Ann James van Hooser, Charlotte, Illinois,1940s.)

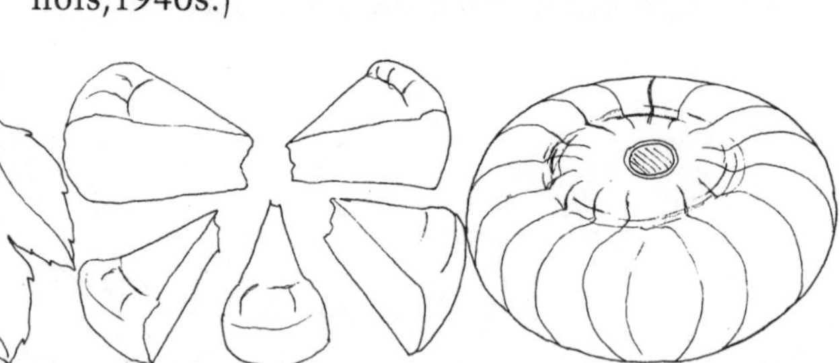

From Shingletown, California, Karen Taylor comments:

My four-year-old concocts soups and teas using leaves, spent flower blossoms, and manzanita berries. He is very serious about his cooking, adding each new ingredient and stirring to blend. (1986)

Small dishes and utensils had to be made for the doll tea parties. A stump table was set with twig ware, leaf plates, nutshell cups, and pine-bark saucers — all displayed on place mats made of woven grasses and flowers.

From Alice Morse Earle: "*Poppy pericarps made famous pepper boxes, from which seed could be shaken as pepper; dishes and cups too for dolls' tea tables and tiny handles of strong grass stems could be affixed to the stems.*"

To play store, children used plants for merchandise. Baskets of berries, boxes of cheese (mallow seed cases), and cans of spinach (crumpled leaves), set out on makeshift shelves, created a grocery store. For money, the shopkeepers used seed pods such as scotch broom (Pat Talbert, California) and eucalyptus (Beverly Elliott, California). If the play store did not realize a profit, no one was disappointed, since all the fun was in setting up the store. Alice Morse Earle also observed that children like to play these imitative games "*with what materials they can obtain, not to have them provided in finished*

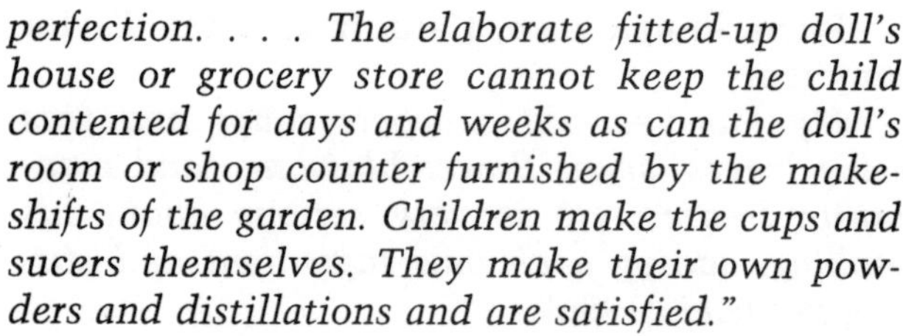

perfection. . . . The elaborate fitted-up doll's house or grocery store cannot keep the child contented for days and weeks as can the doll's room or shop counter furnished by the make-shifts of the garden. Children make the cups and sucers themselves. They make their own powders and distillations and are satisfied."

Let's Make-Believe

Young children lead rich fantasy lives, assuming many roles during one day. Inspired by favorite stories, they turn the back yard into a stage for their plays. Carol Holcomb made believe that her woods were a desert island where she had to fend for herself just like the characters in *Robinson Crusoe* and *The Swiss Family Robinson*. After the bookmobile had made its monthly stop at Barbara Loftus's farm in El Paso, she and her brother would "plak" (play like) the stories from the new batch of books. *"For instance,"* she says, *"if we were playing cowboys, we would describe our clothing, our adventures, and our horses in great detail (my horse was always white with a long wavy mane, and Robert's was always black)."*

Many games were created because of some feature of the garden itself. A long arbor might suggest an arch-roofed cathedral, the road to a castle, or a witch's house. A tall tree might become the crow's nest of a ship sailing to far-off places. *"A very old cedar tree grew in my grandparents' front yard in Pensacola,"* recalls

Carol Holcomb. *"We would pretend that this huge tree was a fortress which protected us from dragons — the cars in the street!"* When Carol visited her aunt in Citronella, Alabama, the garden's formal design suggested the grounds of a castle, so she and her sister became medieval princesses.

Costumes, jewelry, make-up, and disguises to enhance the games of make-believe were ready for the picking. Alice Morse Earle invited her readers to peer into a garden thicket and see *"happy little girls, fantastic in their garden dress. Their hair is hung thick with dandelion curls. . . . Around their necks are childish wampum, strings of dandelion beads or daisy chains. More delicate wreaths for the neck or hair were made from the blossoms of the four o'clock or the petals of phlox. . . . Fuchsias were hung at the ears for eardrops, green leaves were pinned into little capes and bonnets and aprons; foxgloves made dainty children's gloves. "*(1850s)

For Frances Lehde, born in 1912, dressing up was one of the ladylike pastimes for girls. Under the watchful eye of their mother or grandmother, she and her sisters made leaf hats:

Using small twigs we fastened the leaves together. The crown of the hat was formed the same way; strips of leaves across the top and fastened to the band with twigs. Then the decorations were anything we could find — small flowers bunched and fastened like a corsage . . .

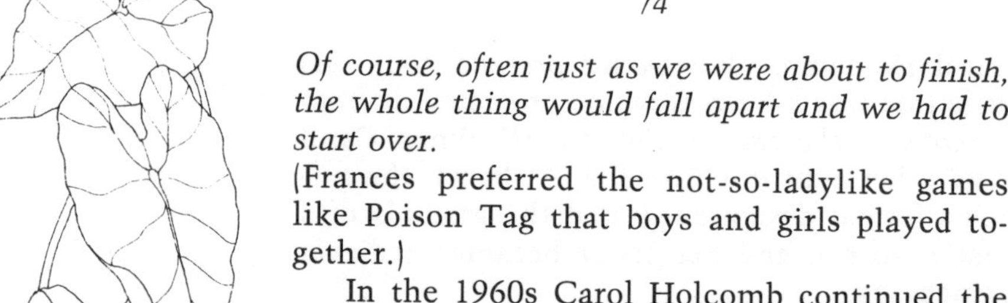

Of course, often just as we were about to finish, the whole thing would fall apart and we had to start over.
(Frances preferred the not-so-ladylike games like Poison Tag that boys and girls played together.)

In the 1960s Carol Holcomb continued the tradition of making leaf clothes. She remembers:

We would sew hats out of leaves we collected off the elephant ear plant [Colocasia], *and sometimes Mother would help us sew together whole dresses from the leaves. We could only do this once or twice though, because if we used all the leaves, the plant could die.*

Vickie Moriarity made hula skirts from feathery weeping willow boughs.

Leaf hats trimmed with flowers and other leaves were part of birthday celebrations at Terra Joann Waters's grandparents' farm in Missouri. Alice Betz remembers a pixie hat worn only on one occasion: *"A night-blooming cactus was in flower; before it closed the next morning, one of my sons picked it and put it on his head."*

Trumpet vine flowers (*Campsis radicans*) made bright orange finger ornaments — "gloves on the ends of ten waggling fingers" (Santmyer, 1900), "elegant fingernails" (Holcomb, 1960s), or "witches' fingers" (York, 1940s).

From Jane Lynch: *"I would rub rose petals on my skin to make perfume."*

From Ann James van Hooser:

As a conservative Mennonite child, I wasn't

allowed make-up, so I "painted" my fingernails with rose petals cut to fit and stained my cheeks and lips with berry juice.

When my brother and I played Indians with our homemade bows and arrows, we raided the chicken coop for feathers. (Dad was a preacher often paid in chickens.) We also picked tomatoes and wore the skins as war paint. Luckily Dad never found out that we had gone into his vegetable garden (forbidden to us except when we helped weed it).

Stringing four o'clocks (*Mirabilis jalapa*) to make colorful ornaments was an approved activity, as Judy Prisley's mother remembers from a 1903 visit she made to relatives in Charleston, South Carolina. She and her cousins, like other proper children, were dressed nicely after their afternoon naps and put out to play until dinner. The bright-colored four o'clocks were just opening when the children came out in the yard. Making different-colored patterns of the flowers strung on broom straw kept the children occupied and tidy until they were called.

When Carole Mitchell was young in the 1950s, *"we used phlox blossoms to make all kinds of wonderful decorations. The long throat on a phlox blossom is inserted into another blossom, and chains are constructed. From these chains we made crowns, necklaces and bracelets."* (Michigan)

Earrings and rings came from an unlikely

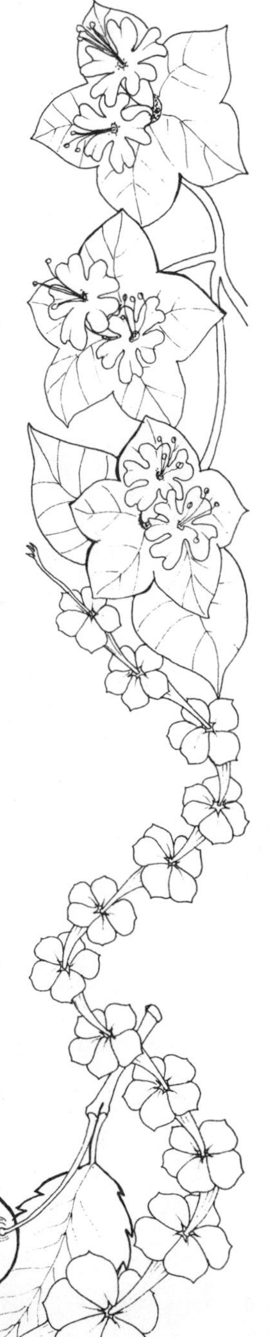

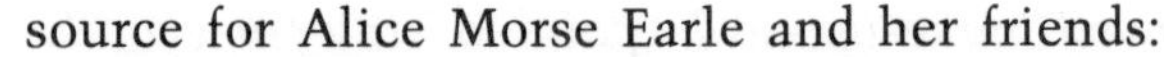

source for Alice Morse Earle and her friends:

The gnarled plum trees at the end of the garden exuded beautiful crystals of gum . . . of which we would say . . . these are my jewels. Translucent topaz and amber were never more beautiful, and, void of setting, these pellucid gems could be stuck directly on the fingers or on the top of the ear. And when . . . we could no longer resist our appetite, there still remained another charm . . . . we swallowed our jewels.

Pat Talbert wore double-connected cherries over her ears for a dangly pair of edible earrings, while Jean Dorrough (San Luis Obispo, California, 1950s) used snapdragons as clip-on earrings.

Terra Joann Waters recalls making necklaces: *"We strung baby pink rosebuds together with thread, added one thin pink ribbon at each end, and made dried necklaces (opera length) to wear during fall and winter."* (1930s)

The most unusual garden jewelry came from insects. Clare Steinfeld recalls, *"We painted the discarded skin-shells of cicadas with water colors and wore them as costume pins."* (Union City, Tennessee, 1930s and 1940s). Jane Lynch adds: "The shell-pins stick to your clothing" (especially a sweater or other rough textured garment). Jane also made rings from the lit-up tail of fireflies, but comments that this seems "gruesome in retrospect." Anne Osia remarks, *"I once saw little girls taking lightning bugs and squishing them as they lit up. They proceeded*

to put the lighted matter on their fingernails. I couldn't bring myself to do it, but it did look unusual." (Bel Air, Maryland, 1960s.)

The Flowers of Summer

In the summer garden a succession of old-fashioned flowers came into bloom. Children's favorite perennials (and biennials) were: hollyhock, canterbury bells, foxglove, larkspur, rose, phlox, honesty, poppy, and the evil (yet fascinating) monkshood. The most remembered annuals were nasturtium, four o'clock, morning glory, snapdragon, and balsam. Each of these plants was associated with a pastime or amusement. Many of the customs were traditional forms of play passed down through generations of children.

Alice Morse Earle, in listing her favorite childhood flowers, begins with *"three noble creatures — Hollyhocks, Canterbury Bells, and Foxgloves. . . . I cannot think of a child's summer in a garden without these old favorites of*

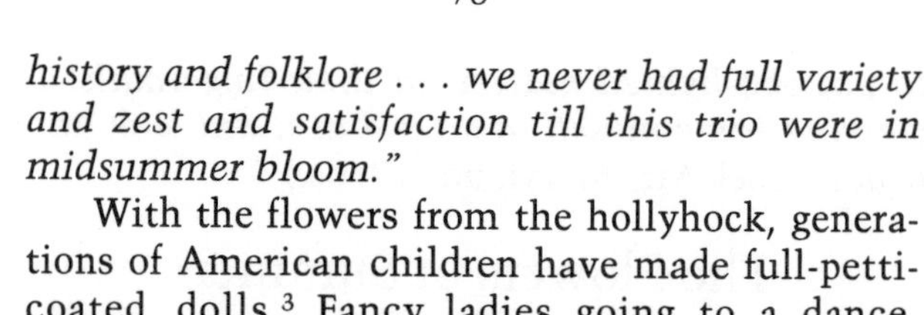

history and folklore . . . we never had full variety and zest and satisfaction till this trio were in midsummer bloom."

With the flowers from the hollyhock, generations of American children have made full-petticoated dolls.[3] Fancy ladies going to a dance, ballerinas on stage, a wedding party, a garden party — such are the games of make-believe and dreams of the future that hollyhock dolls bring to life!

The simplest way to create one of these dolls was to invert a fully opened bloom, as Beverly Elliott did in California in the late 1930s. She "stripped the excess pollen off . . . and twirled them about on the front porch like tops." Some children, like Alice Morse Earle in the 1850s and Terra Waters in the 1940s, tied a bit of string to nip in the waist of the dolls. Many children used a combination of a bud (for the head and hat) and a fully open flower (as the skirt). These dollmakers inserted the stem of the open flower into the base of the bud.

"The small holes at the base of the bud were the eyes and our ballerinas came to life! . . . the stages were our designs and we were the program's choreographer," remembers Ann Ansinn, who created her dancers in Mendota, Illinois, in the 1950s. A fancier doll wore a third bloom, partially opened, for a cape. Some children secured the doll and made arms with a toothpick while Joy Smith put her dolls over clothespins so that they could stand up in sand.

Probably the most delightful way to play with hollyhock dolls was to make them dance on water. Donna Thomas, who grew up in the 1950s, recalls:

When I visited my Cherokee grandmother in Keokuk, Iowa, she would take blossoms and buds from hollyhocks and fashion a fancy lady with a billowing skirt and little hat. Then we placed the lady on the water in the #2 washtub outside on the brick wall overlooking the Mississippi River and I would spin her around on the water's surface and think of the beautiful story by Walt Disney where the boy and the girl danced in the pavilion in the sky and sang about a prince who would come.

Blooms from the canterbury bells also made dainty dolls for a delightful garden game described by Alice Morse Earle:

By the constant trampling of our childish feet the earth at the end of the garden path was hard and smooth under the shadow of the lilac trees near our garden fence; and this hard path, re-

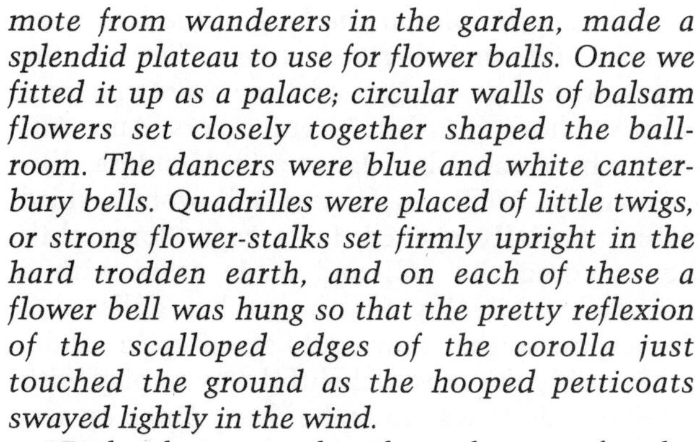

mote from wanderers in the garden, made a splendid plateau to use for flower balls. Once we fitted it up as a palace; circular walls of balsam flowers set closely together shaped the ballroom. The dancers were blue and white canterbury bells. Quadrilles were placed of little twigs, or strong flower-stalks set firmly upright in the hard trodden earth, and on each of these a flower bell was hung so that the pretty reflexion of the scalloped edges of the corolla just touched the ground as the hooped petticoats swayed lightly in the wind.

Earle also remembered another use for the canterbury bells:

There was a little gawky, crudely-shaped wooden doll sold in Worcester which I never saw elsewhere . . . These dolls came in three sizes; the five cent size was a midsummer favorite, because on its featureless head the blossoms of the canterbury bells fitted like a high azure cap. I can see rows of these wooden creatures sitting, thus crowned, stiffly around the trunk of the old Seckel pear tree at a doll's tea party.

Witches' Bells, Fairy Folks' Gloves, and Finger-Flower are only three of "the sixty-two folk names of the foxglove." According to Alice Morse Earle, the multitude of folk names "give ample proof of its closeness to humanity; it is a familiar flower, a home flower." She recalls childhood uses for this beloved flower:

We used to build little columns of foxgloves

by thrusting one within another, alternating purple and white; and we wore them for gloves and placed them for foolscaps [dunce caps] on the heads of tiny dolls.

Little girls growing up on the West Coast made fuchsia dolls. According to Jeannine Emard, *"Fuchsias thrive in the foggy cool climate of San Francisco, and I spent hours making ballerina dolls from them. The stem holding them to the branch became the arms when inserted in the upper body through a small pin hole."* Edna Knudson adds, *"The petals were the fancy skirts and two stamens were left in place for the legs."*

Certain leaves and seed pods were memorable. For example, if you cup a nasturtium leaf in your hand and put in a little water — behold! you have a handful of molten silver. The seed pods of *Impatiens oliveri* were great fun, as Rose-Marie Vassallo-Villaneau explains:

All summer a whole bed of impatiens provided us with endless moments of pleasure with its dehiscent capsules: at the slightest touch they suddenly rolled up, scattering their seeds in every direction! Every day we went and tried our luck among the ripening pods — there were fights when one of us had already "done" every ripe capsule in sight, leaving nothing to the others. (To tell the truth, I still have that plant in my garden now and I must confess I still like to trigger these minute explosions occasionally.)

Larkspur (*Consolida ambigua*) was the only flower that Alice Morse Earle ever pressed:

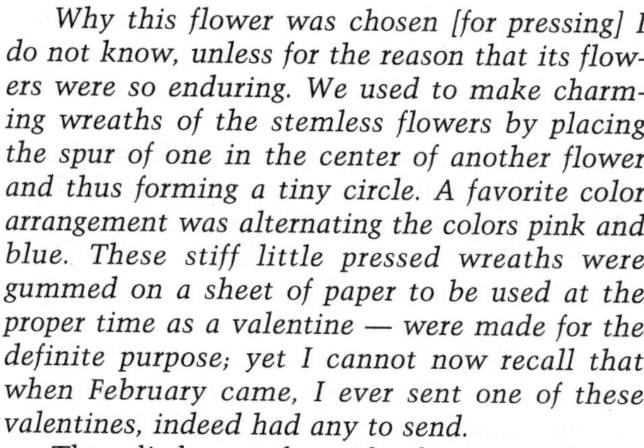

Why this flower was chosen [for pressing] I do not know, unless for the reason that its flowers were so enduring. We used to make charming wreaths of the stemless flowers by placing the spur of one in the center of another flower and thus forming a tiny circle. A favorite color arrangement was alternating the colors pink and blue. These stiff little pressed wreaths were gummed on a sheet of paper to be used at the proper time as a valentine — were made for the definite purpose; yet I cannot now recall that when February came, I ever sent one of these valentines, indeed had any to send.

These little wreaths evidently were traditional, because Earle says: *"I have found these larkspur wreaths in a* Pike's Arithmetic, *used a century ago, and also in old Bibles, sometimes fastened in festoons on the title page."*

The larkspur continued to be a favorite children's flower in the 1940s and 1950s, but for a different reason. As Jane Lynch explains, *"The blossoms looked exactly like tiny rabbit heads in pastel shades of lavender, pink, and white. I used to make up stories about my rabbits."*

Following closely on the heels of Alice Morse Earle's three favorite childhood flowers was a fourth — the rose. Her strongest memories of roses were of their taste, especially in two confections — Rose Tobacco and Rosy-cakes. In her book, *Old Time Gardens,* she writes about a farm in New Hampshire in the late

1800s with a two- or three-acre garden of old-fashioned roses. In the Masons' garden were cinnamon roses (*Rosa cinnamomea*), cabbage roses (*Rosa centifolia*) and pale pink, spicy-scented apothecary roses (*Rosa gallica* 'officianalis'). The neighbors thought this crop a waste of good farm land, but the children in the area rejoiced:

There came every June to this rose garden all the children of the vicinity, bearing milk-pails, homespun bags, and birch baskets to gather rose petals. They nearly all had roses at their homes, but not the Mason roses. These rose petals were carried carefully to each home where they were packed in stone jars with alternate layers of brown or scant maple sugar. Soon all conglomerated into a gummy brown substance, which was known among the children by the unromantic name of Rose Tobacco. This cloying confection was in high repute. It was chipped off and eaten in tiny bits and much treasured as a love token or reward of good behavior.

Similar to Rose Tobacco but more delicate and romantic were Rosy-cakes, also vividly recalled by Earle:

The rose is connected to one of my most tender childhood memories — the making of rosy-cakes. These dainty fairy cakes were made of layers of rose-leaves sprinkled with powdered sugar and cinnamon, and then carefully enfolded in slips of white paper. Sometimes they were

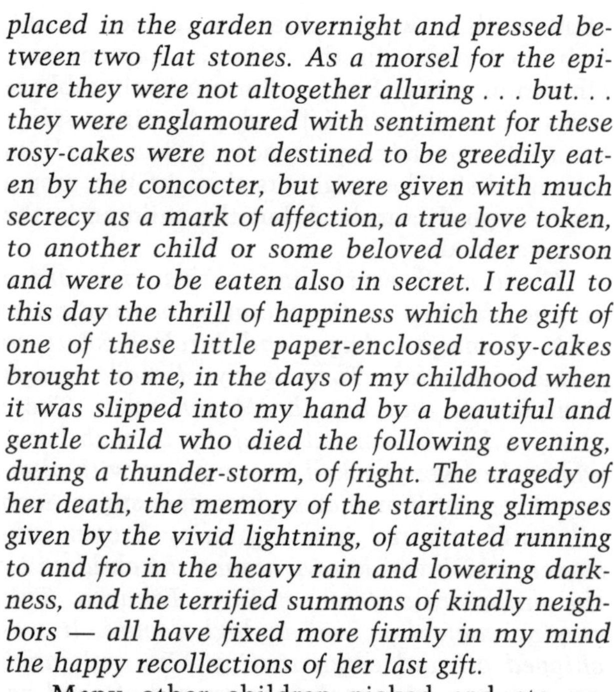

placed in the garden overnight and pressed between two flat stones. As a morsel for the epicure they were not altogether alluring . . . but. . . they were englamoured with sentiment for these rosy-cakes were not destined to be greedily eaten by the concocter, but were given with much secrecy as a mark of affection, a true love token, to another child or some beloved older person and were to be eaten also in secret. I recall to this day the thrill of happiness which the gift of one of these little paper-enclosed rosy-cakes brought to me, in the days of my childhood when it was slipped into my hand by a beautiful and gentle child who died the following evening, during a thunder-storm, of fright. The tragedy of her death, the memory of the startling glimpses given by the vivid lightning, of agitated running to and fro in the heavy rain and lowering darkness, and the terrified summons of kindly neighbors — all have fixed more firmly in my mind the happy recollections of her last gift.

Many other children picked and ate unadorned rose petals. Phyllis Shreves remembers how she and her cousin, Lois, growing up in Texarkana, Texas, would set up their little tea service on the front lawn. She says, *"Since we were pretending to be fairies, we would eat our fairy food — the pink rose petals."* (1940s)

Knowing that the monkshood was poisonous to eat, children warily dissected the flower to find "the devil in his chariot." By taking off the

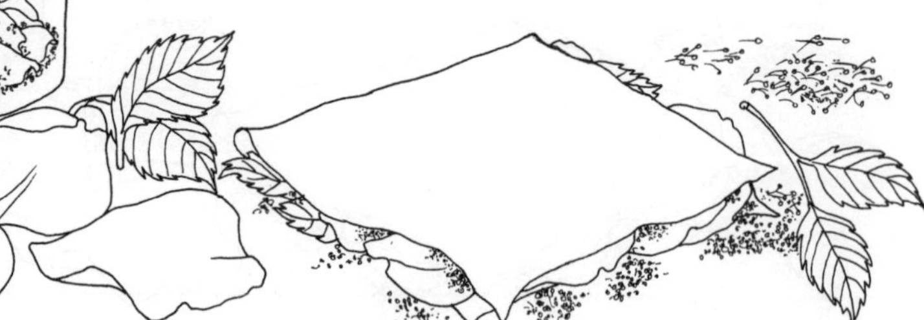

outer layer (the chariot) they uncovered a grizzled Satan: from his wiry hair to the upturned tips of his purple boots, he was a fascinating creature. A cape flared from his shoulders and lavender tights encased his skinny legs. An unlikely name for monkshood — cupid's car — appeard in a list of garden flowers published in Boston in 1828. Similarly, Kerstin Thunmark (Stockholm, Sweden) comments that as a child she learned to pull a monkshood flower apart to find "two doves pulling a shell-shaped car." (Author's note: After puzzling over this, I have tentatively decided that the two doves are the same as Satan's boots; also that the chariot and car are identical.)

Running through the yard, children attacked each other with snapdragons, holding the flower-jaws open and ready to bite. Kristine Davis explains: *"By simply removing one blossom and gently squeezing the sides, the snapdragon will open and then snap shut like a miniature dragon jaw. With some imagination you can even see a tongue and some teeth."* (Whittier, California, 1950s.) When Sandra Bayes squeezed snapdragons, she called it "making the dogs bark," while others have thought the effect was that of a toad opening its mouth.

Peppy Challinor played doctor with morning glories. She says, *"I would pluck one, wrap it in a damp leaf, and treat it with medicine (the milky fluid from its stem)."* (Louisville, Mississippi.)

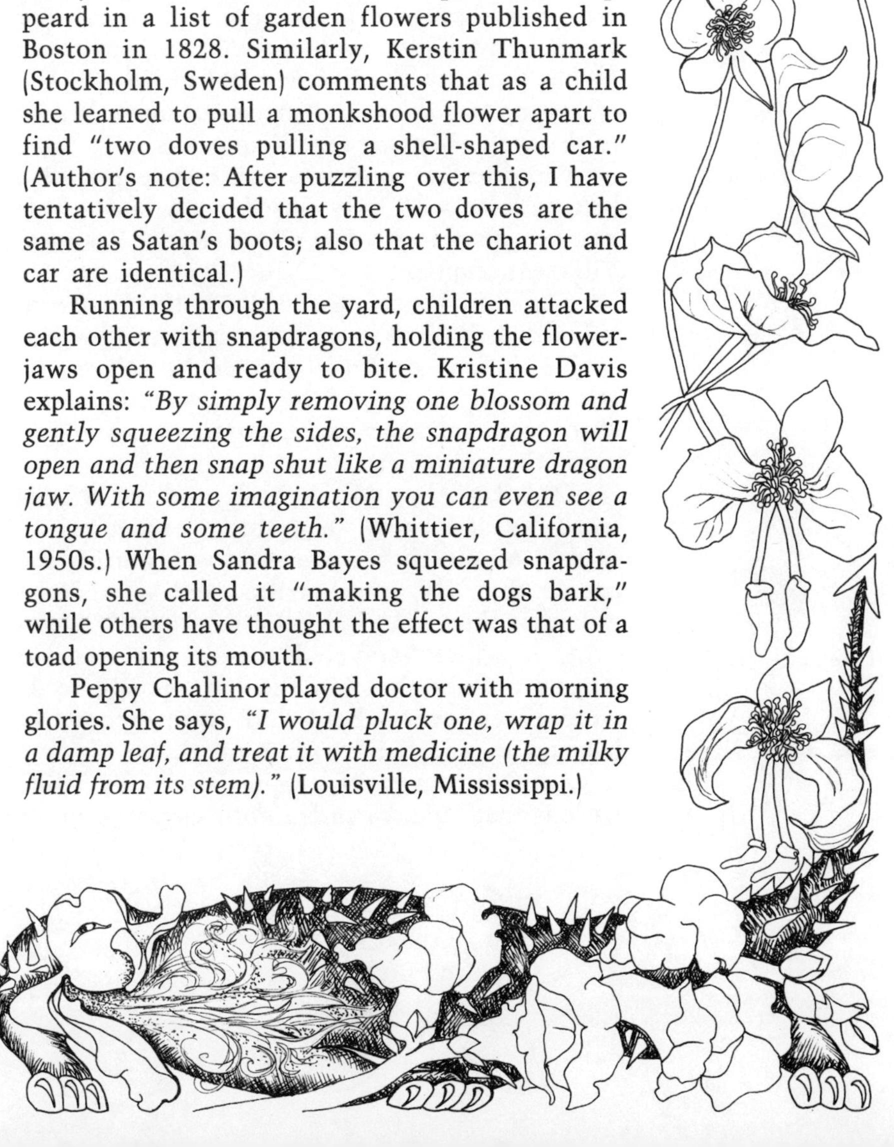

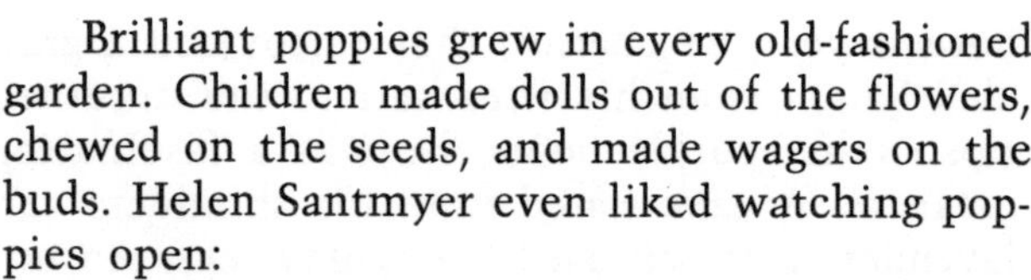

Brilliant poppies grew in every old-fashioned garden. Children made dolls out of the flowers, chewed on the seeds, and made wagers on the buds. Helen Santmyer even liked watching poppies open:

I have more than once sat cross-legged in the grass through a long summer morning and watched without touching while a poppy bud higher than my head slowly but visibly pushed off its cap, unfolded, and shook out like a banner in the sun its flaming vermilion petals.

Children in southwestern France played a betting game with fully closed poppy buds (those not yet showing color). Rose-Marie Vassallo-Villaneau explains:

The aim was to guess whether the flower inside was still white — poulette *(baby chick), pink —* poule *(hen), or already scarlet —* coq *(rooster). Actually the size of the bud gave a hint, still there were surprises and a forfeit to pay if you made the wrong bet.*

One day Alice Morse Earle and her friends were, as she says, "cheerfully eating poppy seeds." An elderly woman, who was visiting the garden that day, was horrified and warned the girls that they would "fall into a stupor."[4] However, a widely traveled missionary assured Alice's mother that "in the East, poppy seeds were eaten everywhere and were frequently baked with wheaten flour into cakes."

Another charm of poppies noted by Alice Earle is that "*black-headed dolls could be made*

from the great poppies, whose reflexed petals formed gay scarlet petticoats."[5] Rachel Hubback remembers how she and her friends made poppy dolls in Cornwall, England:

We cut the stalk short, saving the cut-off part, then folded the petals downwards very carefully so they made a scarlet dress for the doll. This was tied with a sash made from a blade of grass. Then we pricked two eyes, mouth, and nose in the poppy's seedhead, and with the cut-off piece of stalk used part of it to poke through the doll's shoulders to make arms and another part as one leg (the other leg being formed by the attached stem).

In this country poppies were often used to make pin-a-sights, along with ribbon grass (*Pharalis arundinacea* var. *picta*), which was on Alice Morse Earle's list of favorites.

We children used to run to the great plants of striped grass at the end of the garden as to a toy ribbon shop. The long blades of grass looked like some antique gauze ribbons. They were very modish for dolls wear, very pretty to tie up posies, and very useful to shape pin-a-sights.

What were pin-a-sights? According to Earle:

A pin-a-sight was made of a piece of glass on which were stuck flowers in various designs.[6] *Over these flowers was pasted a covering of paper, in which a movable flap could be lifted, to display on payment of a pin, the concealed treasures. I recall as our sights chiefly tiny lark-*

spur wreaths and miniature trees carefully manufactured on grass spires. A noted pin-a-sight, glorious still in childish history and tradition, was made for my pin store by a grown-up girl of fourteen. She cut in twain tiny baskets which she pasted on glass and filled with wonderfully artificial flowers manufactured out of real blossoms. I well remember her "gilding refined gold" by making a gorgeous blue rose out of the petals of a flower-de-luce.

Often several girls would make groups of pin-a-sights (also called poppy shows) and display them on a board. To entice people to come look at their creations, they would chant, "A pin, a pin, a poppy show." Or in other parts of the United States little girls called out, "Pinny, pinny, poppy show. Give me a pin and I'll let you know."

Another way to make a poppy show used two pieces of glass, omitting the paper flap. One woman recalls:

I possessed two pieces of glass, very nearly of a size, between which I used to place fallen poppy petals, in lively kaleidoscopic patterns. I had to hold the glass very tightly not to spoil the pattern by letting them slip. . . .

Some girls carried their poppy shows to school and passed them along under the desks. Other children gave their displays in their barns, and one girl I knew had a tent in which her show was beautifully hidden. . . . It was as exciting as going to a play to lift the [tent] flap and gaze

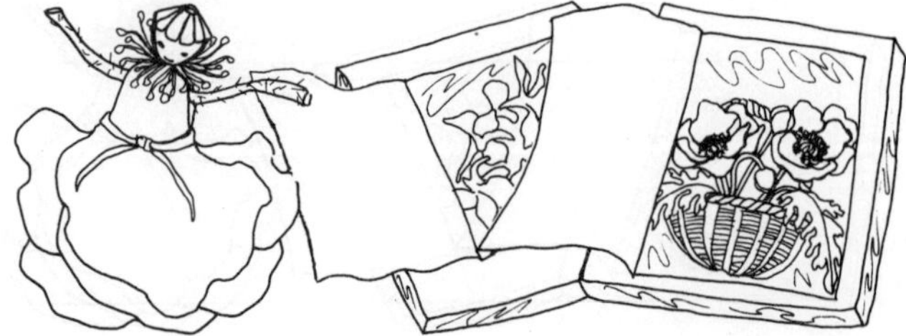

upon the revealed splendors behind the screen.[7]

A variation on the pin-a-sights turned up in Astoria, New York, sixty years later. Jeanné Smith and her friends no longer charged a pin for a look at these "flower graves."[8]

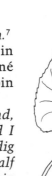

When I was a child I lived on Long Island, where the soil was sandy. My playmates and I would compete with flower graves. We would dig a hole (with our hands) about three and a half inches deep. We would then arrange a flower in the bottom of the hole. Over this we would press a piece of glass and then cover it up with dirt. Then, asking our playmates to view our flower pictures, we would scrape the dirt off the glass in a circular or oval shape and display the "flower graves" we had made. We would decide who had made the best one and then start over again with another hole and different wildflowers.

Sally Wright called these displays "sunken picture gardens" and made them in her sandpile. She placed the flowers on a leaf background, and, after covering the display with the glass, framed it with small stones. The effect, as she remembers it, was like "peering into one of those miraculous diorama Easter eggs."

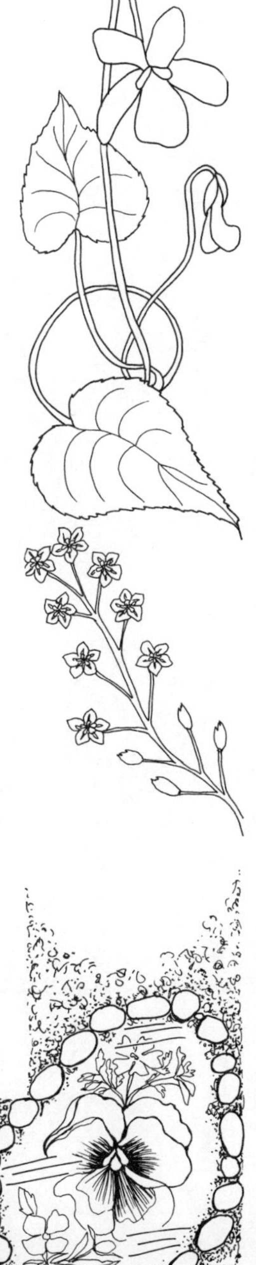

Vegetables

To the imaginative eye, even prosaic vegetables could be fun. Lizz Gilbert, who spent summers in Southbury, Conecticut, says, *"I remember all the funny-shaped potatoes my grandfather pulled from his garden — ducks,*

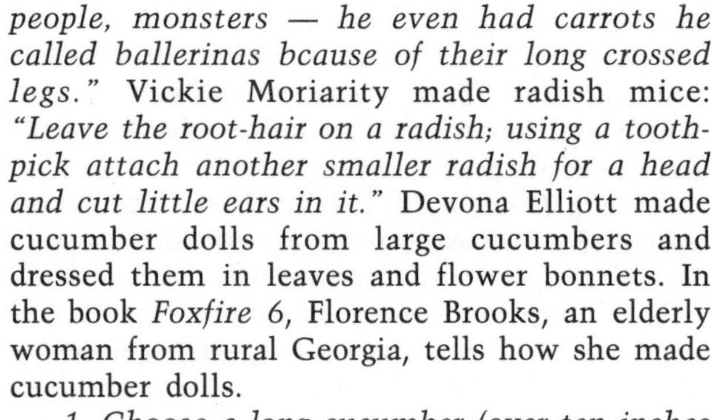

people, monsters — he even had carrots he called ballerinas bcause of their long crossed legs." Vickie Moriarity made radish mice: *"Leave the root-hair on a radish; using a toothpick attach another smaller radish for a head and cut little ears in it."* Devona Elliott made cucumber dolls from large cucumbers and dressed them in leaves and flower bonnets. In the book *Foxfire 6*, Florence Brooks, an elderly woman from rural Georgia, tells how she made cucumber dolls.

1. Choose a long cucumber (over ten inches long).

2. Cut one inch off the end.

3. Scrape out the seeds and pulp up to the place where you will put the mouth.

4. Cut a notch for the mouth, cutting through to where it is hollowed out.

5. With the point of the knife, cut out eyes and a nose. Put little pebbles in the eyes to make them stand out.

6. Pin a diaper around the doll (a square of any cloth, folded into a triangle and pinned.)

7. Make a dress too, if you have the cloth, and wrap it around the cucumber. If you can sew a bit, gather the cloth at one end around the doll's neck.

The main fun in a cucumber doll was in feeding and changing it.

Florence Brooks spooned thin, runny mud into her doll's mouth. The mud ran right through; then, of course, she had to change the diaper.

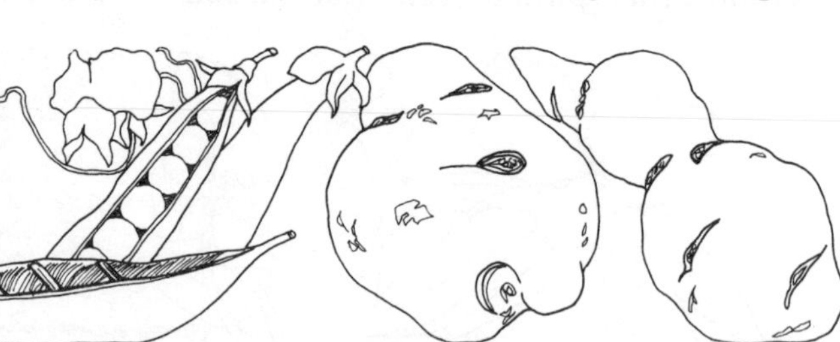

These dolls only lasted a day or two before they turned mushy and attracted fruit flies.

A whole cucumber or zucchini could also be a wagon — Barbara Barnhardt's mother always cut cucumber slices for the wheels (South Carolina, 1930s). Nancy Peiffer made peapod canoes with bits of toothpick for the seats and floated them on a tub of water (Pennsylvania, 1940s). Evelyn Anderson added "pea people" (peas held together with toothpicks) when she made the same canoes in Iowa during the 1920s. Joyce Koldys's brother made squash and cucumber cows and horses when he played farm.

Rose-Marie Vassallo Villaneau recalls how she and her sister also played farm:

On rainy days when we played with our toy farm animals on the kitchen table, we asked Maman *to lend us a cabbage, a lettuce, perhaps a bunch of parsley, to transform into a hill, a forest, or whatever, for our plastic animals to graze.*

Rose Marie's mother, who was from Bordeaux, also taught the children a bit of fun at suppertime:

When we were served young broad beans to eat raw with bread and butter and a sprinkling of salt, we never forgot to incise one of the pods at the level of the first bean very slightly so as to bare the bean inside without cutting into it. We obtained something vaguely evoking a monk

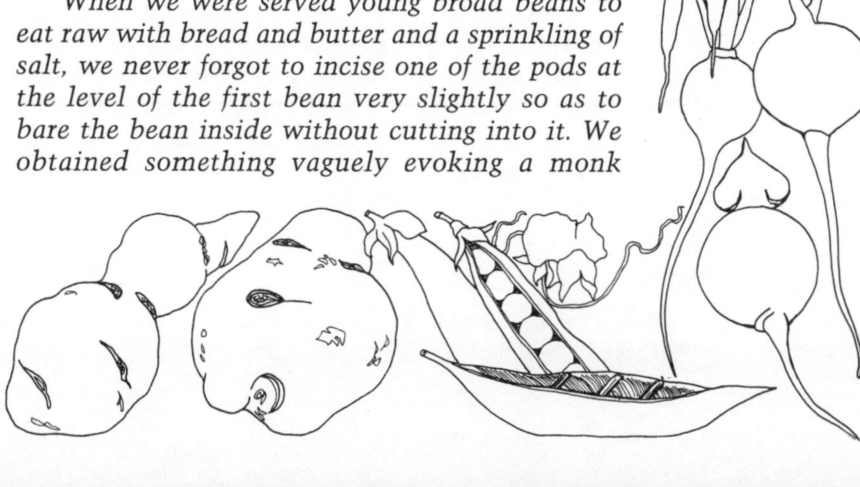

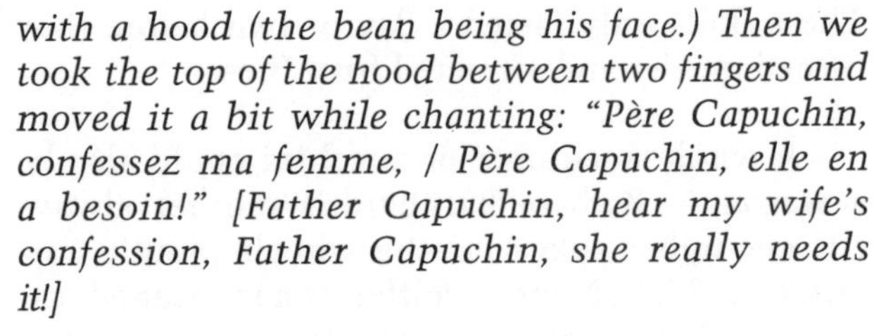

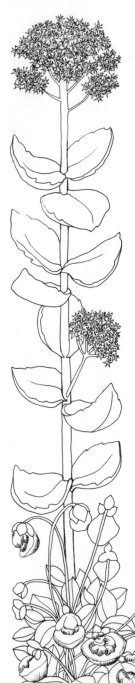

with a hood (the bean being his face.) Then we took the top of the hood between two fingers and moved it a bit while chanting: "Père Capuchin, confessez ma femme, / Père Capuchin, elle en a besoin!" [Father Capuchin, hear my wife's confession, Father Capuchin, she really needs it!]

Making Noise

Many garden plants could be popped or snapped, or made to squeak and squawk. Among those that popped were sedum, morning glory, foxglove, and rose petals. The art of popping sedum leaves was probably ancient when Alice Earle described it, as remembered from her 1860s childhood:

*From the live-forever, or orpine, [*Sedum telephium*] we made frogs, or purses, by gently pinching the fleshy leaves between thumb and forefinger, thus loosening the epidermis on the lower side of the leaf and making a bladder which, when blown up, would burst with a delightful pop. The New England folk names by which this plant is called, such as frog plant, blow-leaf, and pudding-bag plant, show the widespread prevalence of this custom.*

Alice Betz, who grew up in south St. Louis, Missouri, in the twenties also popped sedum leaves, calling them "frog bellies." To LeAnne Arnold they were "puffer bellies," and to Donna Johnson, "balloons." Donna's father taught her how to make these when she was growing up in

Haverhill, Massachusetts. Her balloons were made with the leaves of *Sedum spectabile,* and she explains that you have to "carefully squeeze the leaf until it becomes a dark green. Then its thin green membrane can be separated from the inner leaf tissue. Now blow up and pop!" LeAnne Arnold cautions, "They tear very easily."

Other poppers included the foxglove: *"A rival in sound [to the sedum frogs] could be made by popping the foxglove fingers. English country women call the foxglove a pop."* Alice Morse Earle's comment is confirmed by this quote from Robert Turner, who wrote in 1657:

[The foxglove] . . . is very well known [in Hampshire, England] . . . by the name of poppers because if you hold the broad end of the flower close between your finger and thumb, and blow at the small end, as into a bladder, till it be full of wind, and then suddenly strike it with your other hand, it will give a great crack or pop.[9]

Growing up in California, Jean Rosenfeld used to blow up and pop proud purse (*Calceolaria*). Alice Earle also popped morning glories and canterbury bells.

Rose petals were popped by an altogether different method. From Alice Morse Earle: *"We placed rose petals and certain tender leaves over our lips and drew in the centres for explosion."*

Nelson Coon's 1957 book, *Using Wayside Plants,* also mentions popping leaves and rose

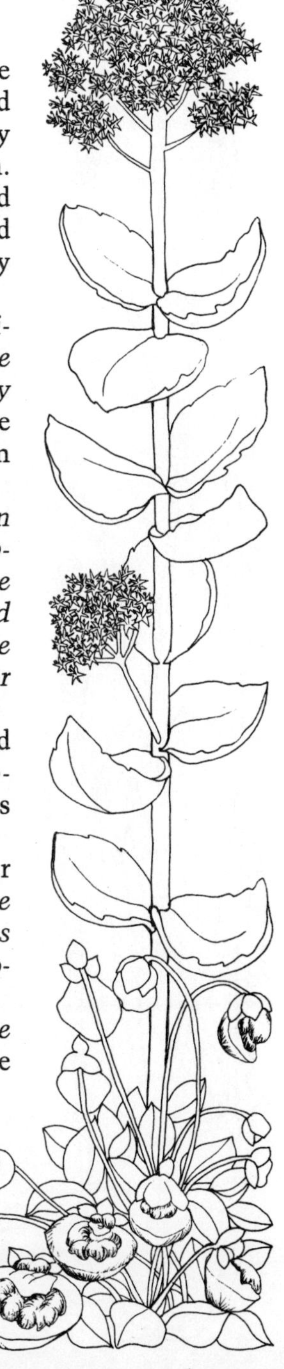

petals. Coon advises the would-be popper to center the leaf over the lips and take a quick, deep breath.

A bovine chorus filled the air when children played on pumpkin leafstalk horns.[10] The longer stems produced deep tones like the moo of a cow, while the shorter stems sounded like bawling calves. (In fact, cows would answer and even approach when they heard this instrument.) Elizabeth Pentecost (now in her seventies) made pumpkin-stem horns as a girl in North Carolina: *Cut a stem of pumpkin or squash with the leaf attached. The cut end will be hollow. Now cut the leaf off, high enough up from its stalk so that the opening is pbstructed. Make a slit in that end about one inch long. Scrape off the prickles around the slit, and blow.*

Almost everyone has heard of whistling through a blade of grass, but not everyone can master the trick. Although many noisy pastimes were reserved for boys in Alice Earle's day, she admits to participating in grass whistling:

A particularly disagreeable sound could be evoked by every boy and (I must acknowledge it) by every girl too, by placing broad leaves of grass—preferably the pretty striped ribbon grass or gardener's garters — between the thumbs and blowing thereon.

Hilda Badger Drummond's father (c. 1917) taught her to hold the grass blade very taut between her side-by-side thumbs. When she blew through the small space, a "lovely harsh crow

sound" came forth. Bob Burrell recalls: "It was a favorite of junior-high types who sneak up behind some unsuspecting girl, scaring the wits out of her," but concedes that it requires a degree of skill to make the sound. He says, "Even today I am only successful about one time out of five." Geoffrey Charlesworth admits he "never mastered that one," but he did enjoy a bit of success with a privet leaf. Privet (*Ligustrum vulgare*) was a common hedge in northern England where Charlesworth grew up. He would pick a privet leaf, fold it over, and then as he explains: "Blow into the top and pull at the bottom to make a nice squeaky instrument." His achievement? "I used to manage 'God Save the King,' first line, before the leaf broke!"

Evening in the Garden

One of the wonderful things about summer is that there is time to play after supper. When evening began to gather about the garden, it was time for games like Ain't No Bears Out Tonight, Squat Tag, and Kick the Can. As the grownups came out to sit and talk, the games quieted down. Sometimes children lay flat in the grass to watch the stars and half-listen to the adult conversation, but mostly to avoid notice in case bedtime might be announced. Mother might take a stroll around the garden and point out the strong nighttime fragrance coming from the yucca plant or tell the kids to watch the evening primroses. Alice Morse Earle remembers:

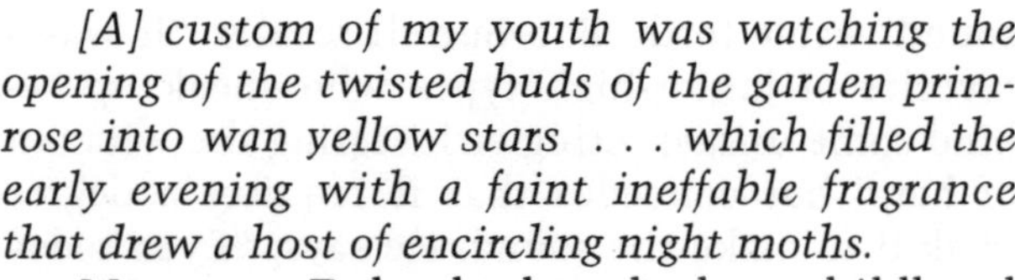

[A] custom of my youth was watching the opening of the twisted buds of the garden primrose into wan yellow stars . . . which filled the early evening with a faint ineffable fragrance that drew a host of encircling night moths.

Margaret Deland shared that childhood memory, for she wrote:

Here, in warm darkness of a night in June,
children came
To watch the primrose blow.
Silent they stood,
Hand in hand, in breathless hush around
And saw her shyly doff her soft green hood
And blossom — with a silken burst of sound!

Alicia Leal and her sister Ann liked to end a summer's day in the 1940s by giving a concert under the stars. After the girls had finished drying and putting away the dishes, they headed for their Colorado back yard to make music.

Our instruments were odd-shaped pipes and pieces of iron. We pinned our "music sheets" (pages from a discarded Sears catalogue) to the wire fence. Our attentive listeners — the tall, graceful hollyhocks lining the fence — swayed in time to our music.

SUMMER AFIELD

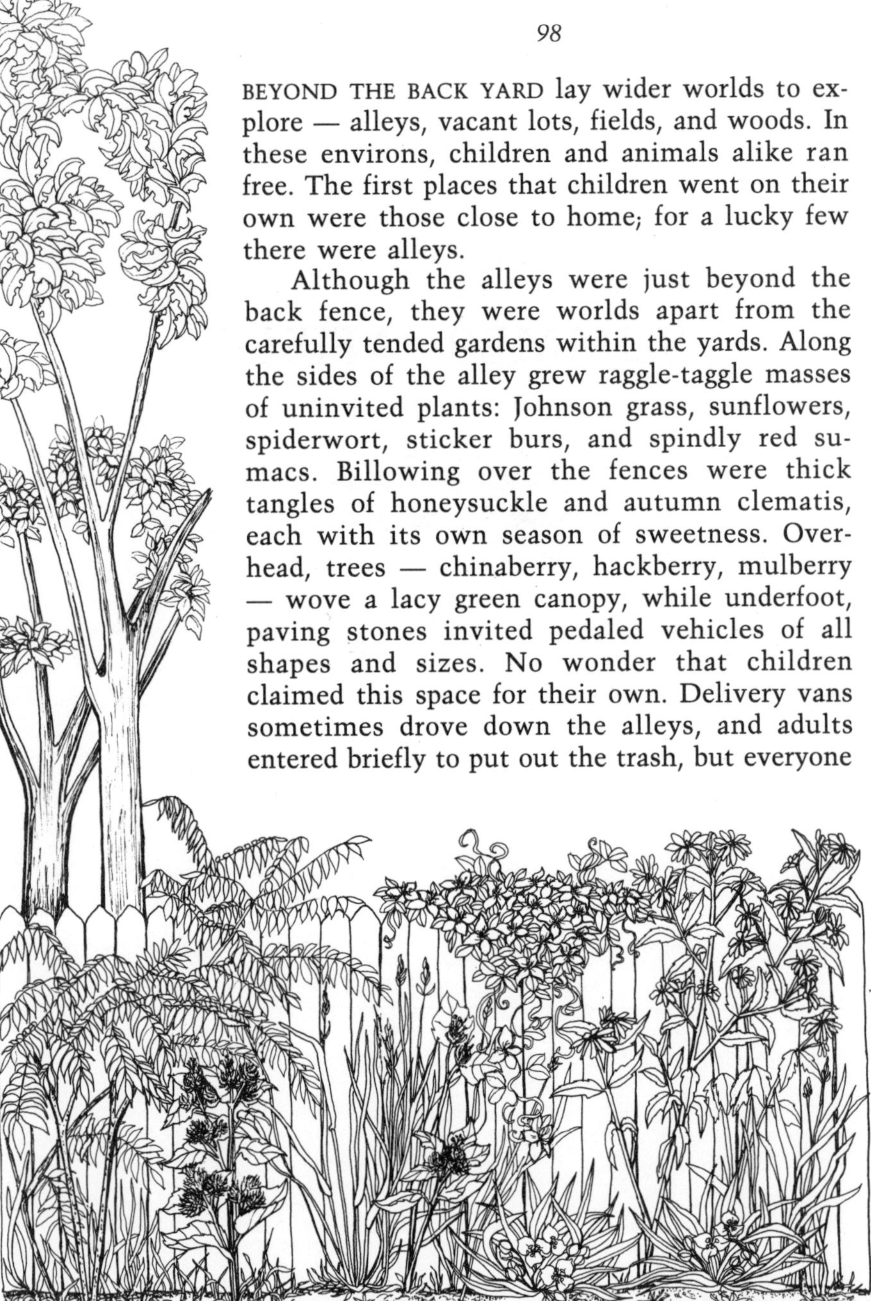

BEYOND THE BACK YARD lay wider worlds to explore — alleys, vacant lots, fields, and woods. In these environs, children and animals alike ran free. The first places that children went on their own were those close to home; for a lucky few there were alleys.

Although the alleys were just beyond the back fence, they were worlds apart from the carefully tended gardens within the yards. Along the sides of the alley grew raggle-taggle masses of uninvited plants: Johnson grass, sunflowers, spiderwort, sticker burs, and spindly red sumacs. Billowing over the fences were thick tangles of honeysuckle and autumn clematis, each with its own season of sweetness. Overhead, trees — chinaberry, hackberry, mulberry — wove a lacy green canopy, while underfoot, paving stones invited pedaled vehicles of all shapes and sizes. No wonder that children claimed this space for their own. Delivery vans sometimes drove down the alleys, and adults entered briefly to put out the trash, but everyone knew that this untamed territory belonged to the children.

For farm children, the first places to explore were on the family acreage. After chores were done, Shirley Pfeifer and her three brothers and sisters would go on expeditions:

Before wandering off, we were to report to our mother our intended destination. We assigned names to the areas of our 120-acre farm — East Forty, Big Pasture, and Little Pasture. In Big Pasture was Big Pond, and in Little Pasture was Little Pond with a creek flowing around it. We often played near the trees that grew along the creek, among their large exposed roots.

Eleanor Leadsom and her brother would often head for the back of their farm in Canada to a fairly large woods with a creek running through. She relates:

To get to the woods we went along a lane bordered on each side with stump fences. The lane led us to the railway track, which we had to cross to get to the woods. We would sit on the

grass in the lane, looking for four-leaf clovers, watching ants, or just daydreaming until a train came. Then we jumped up and waved at the crew. (They always waved back.) Often we tried to count the freight cars. The passenger trains went by too fast to count the cars, especially one that went by at 8:30 P.M. called the Wolverine. We always coaxed to stay up a little longer — just 'til the Wolverine goes by, Mother."

To Evelyn Vincent, *"The happiest privilege we enjoyed was freedom. . . . We went to the woods and roamed all day, just so we got back before dark. Mama let us go in the shallow creek, climb as high as we pleased in the trees, and take all-day hikes the several miles to the lake."*

She also reminisces about one memorable excursion:

Picnics in Shepherd's Pasture were nothing new to us, but this day was marked from the beginning, set apart because Emily's mother had made tea for us and put it in a fruit jar with ice cubes. *(The Woodhams had a new Frigidaire, one of the first refrigerators in town.) We anchored our tea jar in a little hollow by the bank of a stream where we always stopped. Sandwiches and the two apples were safe from ants in a tightly closed syrup bucket. Our rambles that day took us farther into unfamiliar territory than we had ever gone before. Deep in the wooded part of the pasture, we found the Tree—claiming it as ours forever from the first moment we saw*

it. That huge willow, many times bigger than the others that grew along our little stream, leaned accommodatingly over the water, making it easy to walk right up the trunk to the spreading limbs that threw lacy shadows on the clear water below. The Tree was to serve us through many picnics as a house, a stage for our plays, and a ship. Although we had often sailed on an abandoned sawmill in the pasture, the water beneath our newly discovered treeship added a splended note of reality to our voyages.

One of Bob Burrell's rambles took him to a different kind of special tree:

All the kids were fond of the big old Initial Tree. It was way out in the country from the city line near where I lived. I thought it was quite a hike through the woods and fields to get to it, and certainly a secret you didn't divulge to the younger kids in the neighborhood. Generations of kids carved their initials on the soft, smooth bark of the tree. The dates go back many years, and the carving wasn't limited to kids — plenty of teenagers engraved their undying adoration for their one and only with hearts and Xs. *(That tree is still standing now, in a thoroughly citified residential area. The funny thing is that what seemed like miles and miles was only about five or six blocks from my childhood home.)*

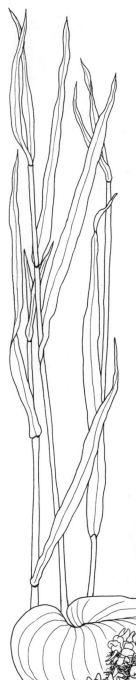

Setting Up Housekeeping

The age-old game of Playing House could be easily adapted to many settings. For example, Kathleen Keefe Bilcz says:

As a child of seven, I spent many happy hours with three other neighborhood children in the vacant lot behind my parents' home in Torrington, Connecticut. The trees and bushes were the roofs of our playhouses, and a row of rocks lined up on the ground made our walls. (1953)

Rose-Marie Vassallo-Villaneau and her sister had their favorite houses in southwestern France

. . . anywhere in the high grass of the orchard before it was scythed (we just trampled down a few square yards and became perfectly invisible); the clumps of reeds by the river (somewhat muddy but otherwise perfect); in the bales of hay or straw of the barn (rather prickly but oh! that fragrance). The great thing about all these houses was that they were small private worlds, places where we could pretend we were independent.

With so many plants at hand, cooking was easy. Kathleen Bilcz recalls:

Our food and dishes were mostly of whatever we found — large leaf plates, tossed salads of mixed greens and berries served with forked sticks. The only store-bought goodies were baking soda and vegetable dyes. We mixed these with water and made fizzy colorful drinks.

"From our pretend grocer I purchased cooked chicken — pieces of damp rotting wood that had the texture and consistency of chicken." (Mim Honkala)

"I pulled off the tiny seed pods of shepherd's purse and used them to feed my tiny dolls. To my eyes they looked like tiny spoons" (Ann Ansinn). Hilda Badger Drummond strewed sweet fern to freshen up the playhouse and served butter-and-eggs blooms for her dolls' breakfasts.

J. Stewart: *"I always used dried dock seeds for coffee. It looks like Maxim freeze-dried instant. I added a bit to a pot or cup of water. Since it does not turn the water brown, this coffee lacks the authenticity of a good cup of mud coffee."*

Plantain seed stalks looked like tiny ears of corn; red sumac heads were meatballs with tomato sauce, and the yellow centers of daisies were pumpkin pies. Judy Corkadel comments: *"I used dried leaves for cornflakes, and grasses and clover for salads. Crushed pokeberries were grape juice, and small flat pieces of wood were used for toast"* (Pennsylvania, early 1960s). Hazel Hawk (Ohio, 1920s) cut up burdock stems for her rhubarb pies.

Bob Burrell also used burdock for rhubarb in his game of farmer. He didn't grow up on a farm, but, as he says, *"I would harvest various weeds and pretend they were vegetables. . . . Does my game sound dumb? Well, it sure beats watching*

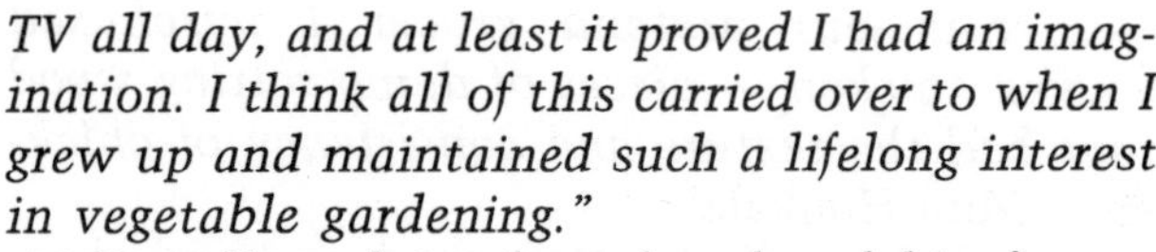

TV all day, and at least it proved I had an imagination. I think all of this carried over to when I grew up and maintained such a lifelong interest in vegetable gardening."

Burrell explains how he played his farmer game:

*Broad-leaved plantain was my beets. The tops looked great, but the roots weren't much. I cut the stalks off large burdock for rhubarb. Ground cherries were my tomatoes (imagine my surprise when years later I found the same plant offered in seed catalogs under the name of husk tomatoes). I saved the heads off both broad-leaved and narrow-leaved plantain and stripped the seeds off for grain. Even though as an eight-year-old I knew no botany, I pretended the Queen Anne's lace roots were carrots. (It was not until many years later than I discovered that our domestic carrots (*Daucus carota sativa*) were probably descended from Queen Anne's lace (*Daucus carota*). I did know that the roots looked just right. Dandelion roots were my parsnips — something we never ate at home, so I don't know where I got this idea.*

On a smaller scale, children made houses for their dolls, or entire tiny towns. Ann James van Hooser recalls:

We dug little pits in the ground for our tiny dolls to live in. They had little dirt shelves to sleep on and their quarters were furnished and

decorated with flowers. Their blankets were any kind of leaf that we could find.

In the 1960s Beth Coleman made villages:

Daddy used to take my sister and me on walks, way down in the woods. We would find a large tree that had lots of moss growing around it. Daddy would show me how to pull up the moss and use sticks to make little moss and wood houses. We would make a whole village and then take little acorns and carve little faces on them for the people. We would play house and laugh for hours. I think the best part was the sharing of love and nature and just being outside.

Clare Steinfeld made "*'fairy houses' in the moss beneath trees with furniture made from sticks, broken glass and other found treasures.*"

In Barbara Barnhardt's tiny villages, the furniture was made from twigs, as were miniature log houses with woven Johnson grass roofs. The furniture was twigs bound together with small lengths of honeysuckle vine.

Among the tiniest of "towns" were the groups of leaf teepees made by Native American children who lived on the Great Plains. They would take one cottonwood leaf, fold it into a tent, and pin the flap with a thorn. After tearing the top a bit to make the smoke-flap, they would set the completed teepee on the ground and go on to make more until there was a whole encampment in miniature. (According to Quinn, who noted these tiny teepees, the children could

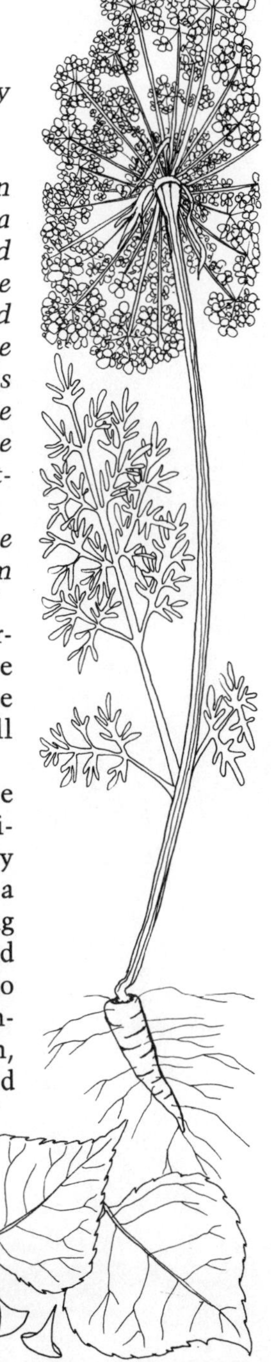

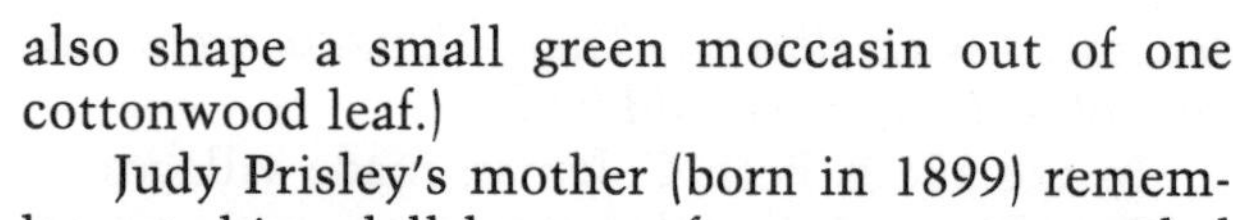

also shape a small green moccasin out of one cottonwood leaf.)

Judy Prisley's mother (born in 1899) remembers making doll houses of many rooms nestled in the above-ground roots of large trees; in the 1950s, Sandra McCann played a similar game:

My sister and I, with the aid of a cousin and two neighbor girls, constructed an elaborate tiny town at the base of an huge old maple tree. Great natural enclosures were formed by its protruding roots. We used twigs, bark, moss, rocks, weeds and any other natural materials we could find to construct our homes and yards. When it was all finished you could travel the streets around a root to the next neighborhood. This tree happened to be in common territory where we were all permitted to play and many hours were spent in improving Tiny Town and trying to outdo each other in creative use of whatever we could find to make our property the best. (Centerburg, Ohio)

Dress-Up was another game that was carried afield. The summer meadows yielded up an abundance of flowers for clothing and jewelry.

*A fresh necklace could be strung from the starry daisy blossoms (*Chrysanthemum leucanthemum*), a daisy chain, just as English children string their true pink and white daisies (*Bellis perennis*).* (Alice Morse Earle, 1860s.)

Sandra Bayes recalls:

We wove and braided flowers and vines into

Indian princess crowns, bride's headdresses (to hold the old lace curtain veil and train), garlands and wreaths. Chicory, Queen Anne's lace, ox-eye daisy, ragged robin, and creeping jenny were good plants for such costumes.

Starr Howington wonders, *"Why did I braid the long three-part pine needles? I guess just to see if I could get the braid all the way to the ends and not separate the top."* Anne K. Osia says, *"Every young hostess wants to be fashionable while giving tea parties. Necklaces as well as rings, bracelets and hats were fashioned of clover. Queen Anne's lace made nice doll placemats and hair decorations.*

This is how Jeanne Frey made her clover chains:

Gather clover blossoms with a two- or three-inch stem. Split the stem about half an inch from the end and thread another stem through it, pulling the blossoms down to the stem. Split the stem of another blossom, pull another blossom through the slit and continue until the chain is as long as you wish it.

After Mary Akstin and her friends had made their clover chains, they would run up to a second-story window and let the chains down to see whose was the longest. (Massachusetts, late 1920s.)

Judy Prisley made crowns, leis, and princess costumes out of periwinkle flowers strung on natal hay stalks. She explains that during the 1940s there were vast spreads of natal hay (*Tri-*

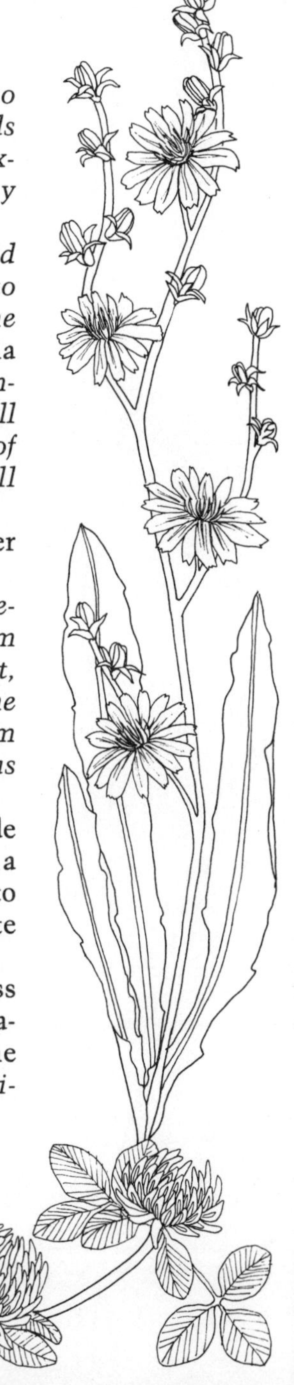

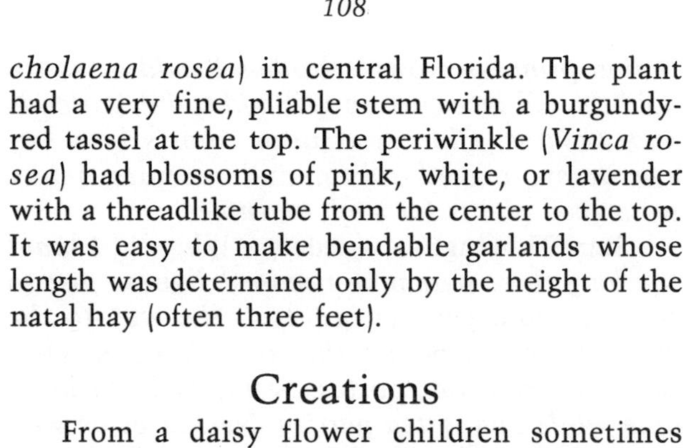

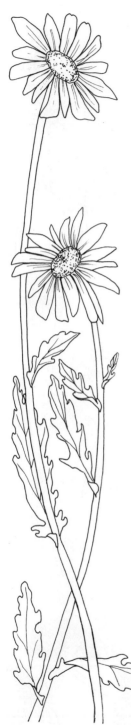

cholaena rosea) in central Florida. The plant had a very fine, pliable stem with a burgundy-red tassel at the top. The periwinkle (*Vinca rosea*) had blossoms of pink, white, or lavender with a threadlike tube from the center to the top. It was easy to make bendable garlands whose length was determined only by the height of the natal hay (often three feet).

Creations

From a daisy flower children sometimes would make a Daisy Grandmother. With their fingernails they shortened all the white rays except two, the bonnet strings, which they left hanging down. On the yellow center they drew a face.

Carol Holcomb made birds' nests out of pine straw. After carefully weaving the needles into the proper shape, she would place her completed nest in a tree. Her only disappointment — no bird ever used these ready-made houses.

Beverly Elliott found a weed with tiny lavender blossoms and long pointed seed pods. She says, *"You pick two seed pods, pierce the center of one with a fingernail, push the other through and the result is doll scissors."* (Jean Rosenfeld, who also did this, says that the plant is a filaree that grows wild in California.)

Bright green spiny burs (with bits of magenta flowers still attached) were, as Alice Morse Earle says, "wrought into interesting shapes," including little baskets:

There was a romance in our neighborhood about a bur-basket. A young man conveyed a written proposal of marriage to his sweetheart reposing in one of the spiny vehicles. . . . I don't know . . . [why] he chose such an extraordinary medium, but the bur-basket was forever after haloed with sentiment.

More prosaic was the furniture that Alice and her friends made for their dolls' houses — tables, chairs, and cradles. They spent hours of pleasure in this fascinating pastime, not deterred by the bits of burs that clung to their clothing. Theresa McCoy, one of eleven children, remembers playing with burs in Illinois:

When the berry season was over and it was too hot or too dangerous (snakes, you know, love hot days) to go walking, we would gather those little stickers that always seem to cling to one's clothes when walking the lanes and paths. The little round ones — I don't believe I ever knew their real names. We just called them stickers.

Well, with a big pile of them we would spend many hours trying to outdo each other with our designs. We made doll house furniture, playground equipment like slides and swings. And then we would try our hand in shaping up dogs and horses, and finally a fence to surround the whole thing. When we had enough, we also put up walls for a house of sorts. (There was another sticker that was about three or four inches long and not very thick. That too was sometimes incorporated into our designs.)

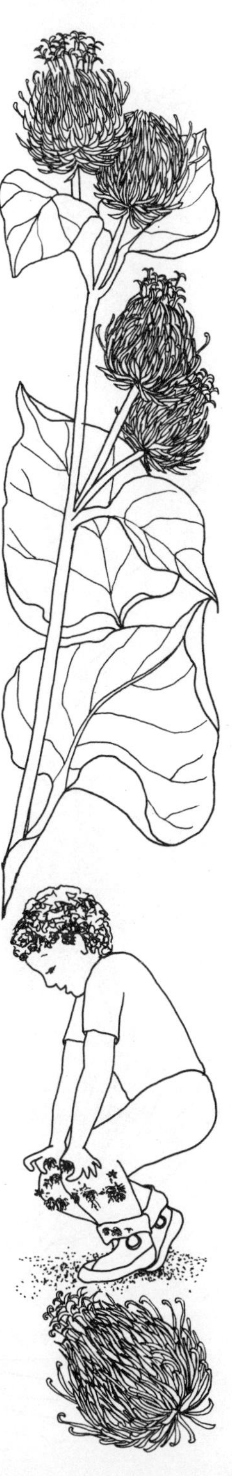

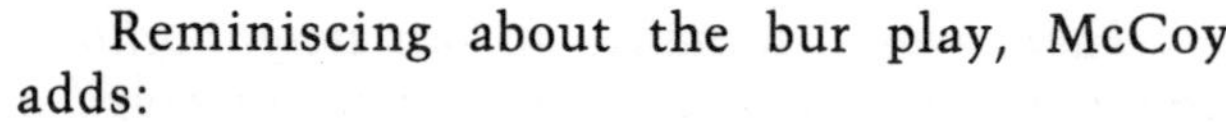

Reminiscing about the bur play, McCoy adds:

These were some of the best summer days we had . . . no need to go around looking for ways to spend money and time. Lazy summer days with some of the best brothers and sisters around. There may have been, but I do not remember, quarrels at those times. (1930s)

Games

The woods and fields sometimes resounded with the shrieks and shouts of vigorous games. For example, a game that Lizz Gilbert remembers took place deep in the woods on the side of a deep leaf-covered ravine. There the Tarzan vines grew — grapevines at least an inch and a half thick. A couple of the stout vines dangled from a tree near a large boulder (the launching pad). She describes the game:

We would climb up on the boulder and someone would swing a vine toward us to catch. Then we would wrap our legs around the vine, getting a toehold in its rough, shaggy bark. Then we would back up to the end of the boulder and, hanging on for dear life, fly off the rock over the slope of the ravine, all the while yelling, "aa-ee-aa-ee-aa" like Tarzan. When we swung out over a big pile of leaves, we'd let go and fall in! (1960s)

For Judy Prisley, the happiest and most enduring game was Cowboys and Indians. She

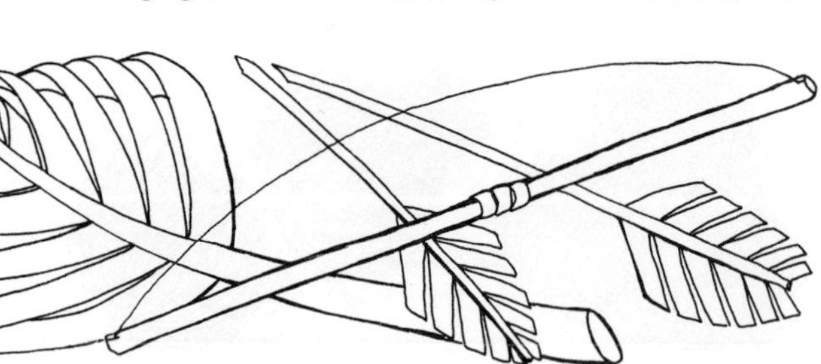

and her boon companions, three brothers who lived nearby, roamed barefoot and dusty in search of raw materials for the Indian part of the game: mulberry branches for the bows and palmetto stalks for the arrows. The children all knew how to care for and use a hunting knife, essential to this craft. Judy explains:

We'd find the straightest possible mulberry branch approximately the diameter of an adult middle finger and cut if off at about a four-foot length. Stripping the bark off left a smooth, white, moist length that we'd notch at each end and string with a tough twine to make a bow. Often we experimented with seasoning the mulberry branch and shaping it by tying it in a curve to a tree or fence post. A strip of rag or a length of adhesive tape wrapped around the mid-section of the bow made a hand grip.

Now for the arrows: palmettos grew in huge clumps at varying heights, each individual stalk being slightly triangular in shape. Again, we'd find the straightest possible branch and cut it from the clump. We'd then whittle it into a point at the root end, shave off the sawtoothed edges of the shaft and trim the built-in feather. (The frond end of the palmetto fanned out stiffly in a palmlike fashion and with the knives could be trimmed closely in a round, ovoid, or triangular shape to simulate a feather, which we then fitted to the twine on the bow for shooting.) We actually could be fairly accurate in target shooting with our homemade bows and arrows.

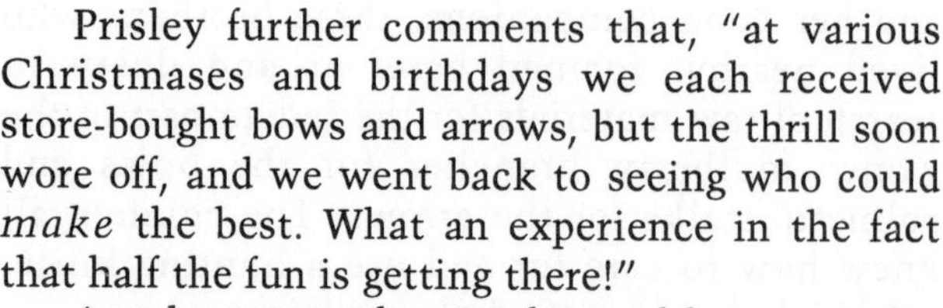

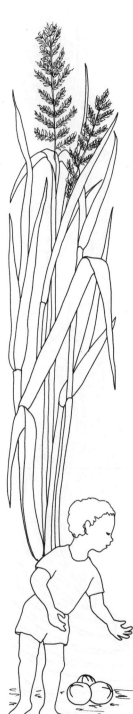

Prisley further comments that, "at various Christmases and birthdays we each received store-bought bows and arrows, but the thrill soon wore off, and we went back to seeing who could *make* the best. What an experience in the fact that half the fun is getting there!"

Another game that Prisley and her comrades invented was similar to bocce or lawn-bowling:

Growing wild in the fields of central Florida were inedible melons we called citron. (I don't know if they were the same thing used for the fruitcake ingredient or not, but to Floridians they were useless.) They were quite round, with smooth white to green skin, about the size of honeydew melons. We used them as bowling balls to have contests of who could roll theirs farthest on the ground toward a specific marker.

"What great fun our twig races were!" recalls Mary Vann. *"We would break open the blisters on small balsam twigs and get fueled up for races on water. The sap propelled the sticks — usually in erratic circles!"* (Smoke Lake, Algonquin Park, Ontario; 1960s.)

Sally Getty (born 1944) relates:

The tall, dry-stemmed weeds in the woods with feathery tops made wonderful spears. Riding on our ponies, we'd be knights — or sometimes Indians, with our dogs as the buffalo. If you threw the spears just right, they would fly forever on the wind. Because they were light, they were harmless to throw at each other — just great fun.

Pranks

When playing pranks on one another, children often used plants. Hilda Badger Drummond asks, "Did you ever use the following mischievous trick to fool an unsuspecting playmate? We did it as part of an initiation ritual into our club."

If you took three or four long stalks of dried grasses, lined them up very neatly and lined up another set of three or four facing in the opposite direction, you then had a bundle of stalks at each end with a clear space in the middle. You then asked the unsuspecting victim to gently *clamp his teeth over the clear space to see what happens. Of course, what happened was a quick jerk of both ends, which immediately [left] the initiate with a very fuzzy mouthful. This was how we tested who was a good sport and who was not.* (c. 1920)

Sheila Silvus Chesanow, who grew up on a farm in West Virginia, recalls a variation on this trick. She and her friends would say to one another, "Let's build a bird's nest." And to the victim, "Would you like to help us build the nest?" When the answer was yes, the perpetrators put fuzzy-ended grasses in the initiate's mouth while saying, "This is how we start to build the nest. You just hold these in your mouth." Then one of the pranksters pulled the ends of the grasses, leaving a fuzzy-mouthed victim, while the spectators collapsed in laughter.

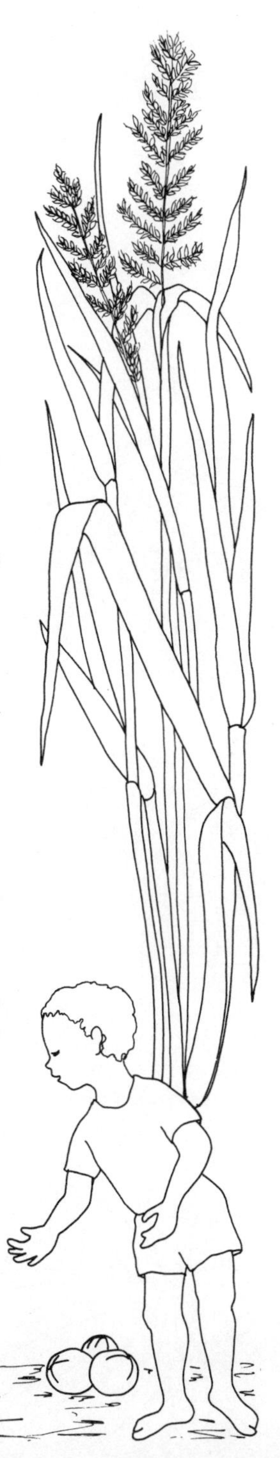

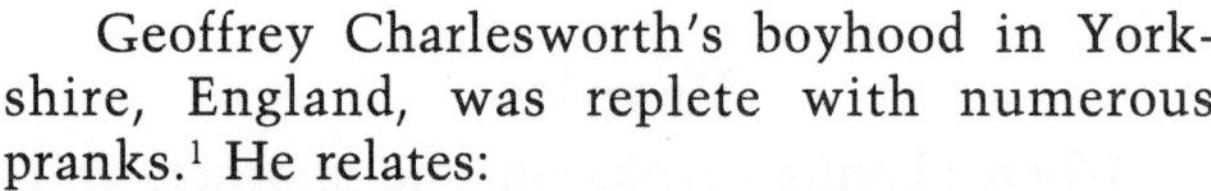

Geoffrey Charlesworth's boyhood in Yorkshire, England, was replete with numerous pranks.[1] He relates:

*There is a grass I haven't seen in the United States which ripens so that the seed strips off the head with a little upward pull, leaving stalklets. You put this in the hair of your friend/foe, twist it a couple of turns, and pull. Mildly painful. Another hostile act is to split open a large rose hip and put the hairy seed down the back of the shirt or dress of a dear one. The resultant itching usually required partial undress for relief. Not quite so irritating, but definitely prankish, is to throw burs on someone's back, or goosegrass (*Galium aparine*), a bedstraw which has hooked stems and hangs onto one's victim in long chains. Nettles were used for very hostile acts, as the sting is quite painful. Wherever you found stinging nettles you could usually find dock leaves (*Rumex crispa*), which would soothe the sting.*

Another remedy for nettle sting comes from Rexine Cardin, who advises, "Pee on it. This really works." (Louisiana)

Bob Burrell played a trick with the seed pods from jewellweed (*Impatiens pallida*). This native plant is also called snapweed and touch-me-not, names befitting Bob's prank. Burrell explains:

It is a minor art form to be able to pick the ripest, most swollen pods without bursting them. Let them lie in your outstretched hand, preferably near the face of an unsuspecting green-

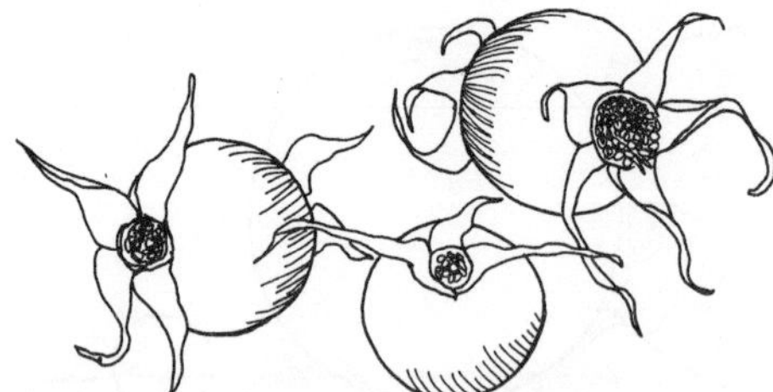

horn. As the moisture and warmth from your hand further stress the tightly stretched seed-pod cover, Pow! The pod explodes, sending seeds into the face of the surprised onlooker.

Some children would hold onto the seed pods, letting them burst within their closed hand just to feel the crawling sensation; others said to a friend, "Would you like to hold my pet caterpillar?" and handed over the seed pods so that their friend could experience the tickling. They advised, "Hold him tight, and you'll feel him crawl."

Pranks sometimes were directed at passing cars. Carol Holcomb remembers a couple:

We would pick the blue berries off an old cedar tree and lob them toward cars that went by. Of course this wasn't as harmless as our other activities, and when our parents caught us at it we were usually dragged inside. Wet pine cones were also excellent missiles, but when I hit a car with one one day and the driver actually stopped and backed up and started to get out of the car, I ran for life. That was the end of the wet pine cones. (Pensacola, Florida, 1950s.)

Clare Steinfeld, growing up in Union City, Tennessee, did this clover-chain trick, as did Jenilu and Addisu Richie, of Memphis. Jenilu recalls:

My sister and I would tie clover stems and blossoms together to make a chain long enough to go across the road near our house. We waited, one on each side of the road, until we saw a

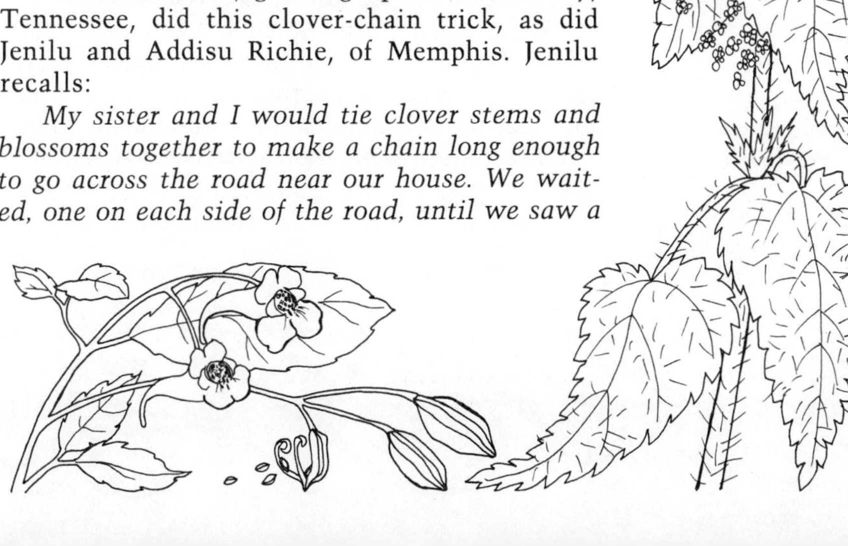

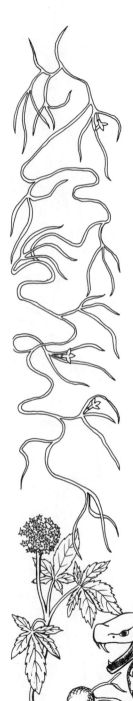

car coming. Then we would hold the chain up and delightedly watch the car break through it. When the car had gone out of sight, we would creep out, get our chain, mend it, and take our positions ready for the next car. I don't believe that Mother ever knew we did this. (1940s)

Earning Money

The first money that Judy Prisley earned outside of family chores came from picking Spanish moss:

Working together, three boys and I kept all the oak trees surrounding our homes stripped clean of Spanish moss as high as we could climb. A croaker sack (burlap bag) over half as high as we were, stuffed tightly with moss, earned twenty-five cents. To sell it, we dragged the bags or used a wagon — or, at the best, persuaded a parent to carry the messy stuff in the car (at the risk of redbugs)—about three-quarters of a mile down a dirt road to where a home business family would spread it out on drying racks and later sell it to be used in stuffing cheap mattresses. It had almost the texture, but not the durability, of horsehair. (Florida, 1940s)

Bill Johnson, who spent his boyhood in the Laurel Highlands region of Pennsylvania, relates that the gathering of ginseng and golden seal provided small amounts of income for the kids:

The older gatherers, the men, realized a far greater income from this activity. Any attempt on the part of the young fry in trying to trail

these pros never met with success. Wild tales of copperheads and rattlesnakes in certain locations were a deliberate effort on their part to discourage juvenile encroachment. (. . . [T]hat these reptiles did, in fact, exist throughout these mountains further buttressed [their] exaggerated claims.)

Carol Holcomb's picking brought in money, but was not an entirely happy experience. Her aunt in Citronella, Alabama, had a huge tree with worms all over it that she sold for fish bait. Carol says:

I don't know to this day what kind of tree it was, but we were paid one cent for each five worms that we would pick for her and put in the bucket. I never did enjoy touching the worms, but the money was nice.

Sara Nelson and her sister went around their California neighborhood picking flowers and making small bouquets. Then, as Nelson comments, *"We would tie these up with ribbon or string and go sell them to the neighbors for a few pennies. It never occurred to us that we were selling the neighbors their own flowers (with short stems and in a faded state); we just thought the whole enterprise was very important."*

When Lori Hayes was ten, she made some "wine" from the chokecherries (*Prunus virginiana*) of a neighbor's tree. *"I used jars, sugar, and about two weeks' patience,"* she recalls. *"Believe it or not, I sold a couple of cups of the vinegarlike punch."*

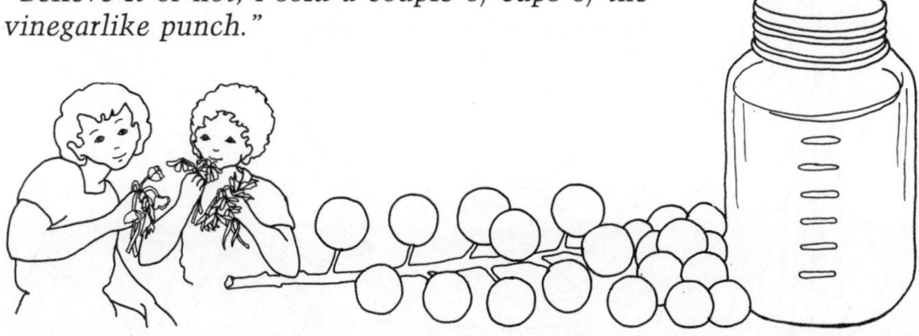

Superstitions

On their summer rambles children found plants to wish on, to pick for good luck, or to ask questions of. For example, to get answers to questions about love and marriage, they consulted daisies, black-eyed susans, bachelor's buttons, tufts of grass, and the love vine.

Alice Morse Earle picked daisy petals in the 1850s, as did seven-year-old Valerie Atwell in 1986, both reciting the same words: "He loves me. He loves me not," until the last petal gave the answer.[2] Lila Ritter used black-eyed susans to get her reply. To find out when you would be married, you said these words while picking the petals: "This year, next year, sometime, never." To find out heir husband's occupation via the daisy petals, girls would chant:

Rich man, poor man, beggar man, thief.
Doctor, lawyer, Indian chief.[3]

J. Stewart remembers playing this fortune-telling game:

We always used buttons for this rhyme. If you came to school with a new dress on or a cardigan sweater (anything with a lot of buttons) one of your friends was sure to rush up and begin, "Rich man, poor man, etc.," starting with your top button. If it ended up badly (with thief, *for example) you could cast about frantically for another button. You might pull up your sweater to show a button on your waistband, which would make your husband a doctor rather than a thief.*

We had an alternate second line to the rhyme, which could change the prediction to "Doctor, lawyer, merchant, chief." Often we would begin again with the top button to find out what the bride would wear ("Silk, satin, calico, rags") and the kind of house she would live in ("Big house, little house, pigpen, barn").

In his book, *Games and Songs of American Children,* Newell mentions a fourth prediction, the wedding vehicle: "Coach, wagon, wheelbarrow, chaise." Originally, boys also consulted their buttons to determine their future occupations; one of Newell's friends had his buttons changed to assure a favorable reading. English schoolboys in the 1770s, using the buttons on a new coat or waistcoat, would say: *"Sowja, sailor, tinker, tailor,/ Gentleman, apothecary, plowboy, thief."* Or, in another version still recited by English children: *"Tinker, tailor, soldier, sailor. / Rich man, poor man, beggar man, thief."*

(In addition to buttons, English girls use beads on a necklace, fruit pits, and seeds on a stalk of dogtail grass.)

A third flower associated with this custom is the bachelor's button (*Centaurea cyanus*). A poem, *Decision of the Flower,* refers to the practice:

Now, gentle flower, I pray thee tell
If my lover loves me and loves me well;
So may the fall of the morning dew
Keep the sun from fading thy tender blue,
Now I number the leaves for my lot,

He loves me not. He loves me. He loves me not.
He loves me. Yes! thou last leaf, yes!
I'll pluck thee not for the last sweet guess.
(Letitia Elizabeth Landon, 1802-1838.)

Young men would pick a blossom of bachelor's button early in the morning and put it in their pocket. If, twenty-four hours later, the color was still bright, she would be "true blue" to him.

Frances Lehde, who grew up in Kentucky in the 1920s, recalls another way to tell if someone loved you:

Dodder, a parasitic vine, grew in the pastures. It had no roots but took its sustenance from other plants. It was a coral-red tangled mass — we called it love vine, and tried to tie a love-knot. First we had to untangle a piece of vine long enough to tie a knot (no easy task given the texture of the vine); then we tied the knot, after dedicating it to the object of our affection. If the knot could be tied without breaking, "He loved me." If it broke (as it usually did) before the knot was pulled tight, "He loved me not."

Four-leaf clovers were good luck. Children saved these to take home and press in a book or they put them in their shoe.

Four leaf clover in my shoe,
Please to make my wish come true.[4]

If you wanted to find out how many lies you had told recently, a plantain leaf could reveal the secret. According to Eleanor Leadsom (Till-

sonburg, Ontario), who did this in the 1920s, *"When the plantain leaves were a good size, we pulled them off and counted the threads that hung from the end of the stem. This was the number of lies."*

Rexine Cardin's grandmother taught her a way of predicting the future with a clover blossom:

I would pick a red clover blossom, spit on it, and toss it over my shoulder. Then I would take ten steps backward, dig a little hole, and there (if it worked out) I was supposed to find a hair, being the same color as the hair of the man I would someday marry. (Northern Louisiana, late 1950s.)

Something that was lucky but rarely found was a fairy ring — a full circle of mushrooms growing in a field. A certain fungus was also lucky, according to Rose-Marie Vassallo-Villaneau, who says:

When you found this fungus, a tiny scarlet cup growing on dead wood [a variety of Peziza, *perhaps], not only were you sure to be happy and rich a whole year long, but moreover you were allowed to offer it to whomever you wanted, and that person was supposed to make pancakes for you!*

Seeds also were reputed to have unusual powers, but as omens rather than as good luck charms. Rose-Marie and her friends practiced seed divination:

Throwing in the air a handful of certain

*seeds and trying to catch them again was supposed to answer questions. The number of seeds told you, for example, how many years you had to live. The answer was usually "plenty" unless a gust of wind spoiled everything. Some seeds we used for this were: cock's foot (*Dactylis glomerata*), soft chess (*Bromus mollis*) and curly dock (*Rumex crispus*).* (France, 1950s.)

In the United States, girls picked apart the yellow seeds from a daisy, threw them up, and tried to catch them on the back of one hand. The number caught predicted how many children each would have.

Children made wishes on the evening star, a flock of birds, or a wagon or truckload of hay. They would say, *"Load of hay, load of hay / Make a wish and turn away."*(If you looked again at the load of hay, your wish would not come true.)

A wishing tree was one with a low branch extending at a right angle to the trunk and making another right angle upward to form a seat. If you sat in this wishing seat while making a wish, it was sure to come true.

It was bad luck to eat certain combinations of foods. For example, Kim Standard, of Atlanta, says, *"If one eats watermelon and drinks beer at the same time, he'll die."* And Beverly Elliott (California) comments, *"It was a known fact that eating cherries and drinking milk at the same time was deadly poison."* Being of an inquiring turn of mind, she decided to test this bit of folk wisdom:

I still remember taking a jar of milk up into a cherry tree and sipping and munching alternately (in a spirit of inquiry not despair) and being somewhat disappointed when nothing happened!

The Five Senses

The sights, sounds, smells, tastes, and textures of early childhood remain in one's memory, often connected to strong emotions and images. For many, these first sensory memories are of familiar childhood plants.

Walking the woods and fields near home, children would chew a stalk of timothy grass, recoil from the sting of a nettle, and inhale the freshness of a hay-scented fern. Other plants, compelling in their color or shape, invited scrutiny.

Sights

Two flowers, so tiny as to be almost inconspicuous, attracted Rose-Marie Vassallo-Villaneau, who muses:

If I were allowed a single word to sum up my childhood relationship with plants, I'd choose fascination. Many plants engraved on my memory from those early days were not playthings but objects of contemplation. Oh, the perfection of the bright scarlet pimpernel, the true-blue bird's eye, the intriguing pennywort. I remember looking into them and nearly entering them, as if I were an insect! . . . Young children seem to be more sensitive than adults to the lure of minute

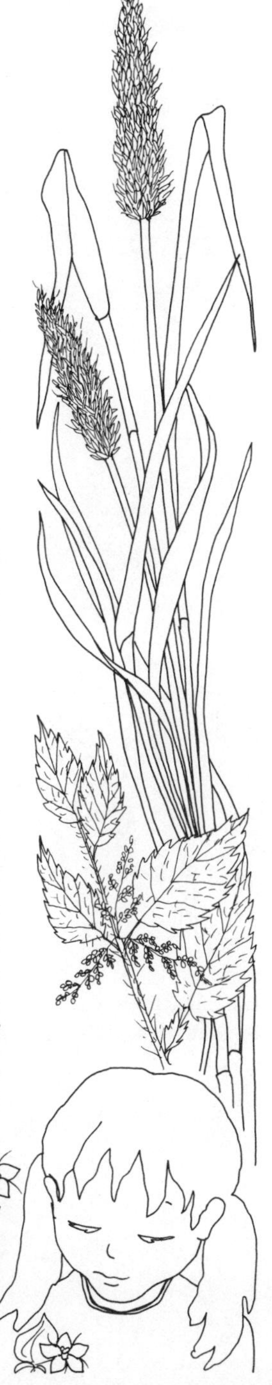

flowers — perhaps either because their eyes are not so far from the ground or because they abandon themselves more unrestrainedly to fascination with small things.

Queen Anne's lace became part of another child's fanciful thoughts. As she stared into the heart of each lacy flower, Elizabeth Austen pondered:

It does *look like lace . . . so fine . . . Nobody could really make lace that fine . . . It has a fuzzy look too . . . What's that in the middle? If this is the queen's lace, than that in the center must be a jewel . . . a jewel like queens and princesses wear . . . These jewels come in different colors . . . I see red and black, wonder if there are any other colors . . . Here's one without a jewel, not very lucky . . . The red ones could be rubies and the black ones could be . . . what is the black stone in Daddy's ring? Onyx, that's it. The black ones will be onyx . . . Rubies are better . . . Whenever I see Queen Anne's lace from now on, I'm going to look for the ones with the rubies in the middle . . . those are the best and rarest . . . If I see a ruby, it will bring me luck.* (1940s)

Jewelweed (*Impatiens capensis* and *I. pallida*) has spotted flowers shaped like a fireman's hat, "jet-propelled" seeds, and leaves that become diamond-encrusted with dew. *"When you hold a jewelweed leaf upside down under water, it turns to silver,"* says Anne Braman, who grew up in Stratford, Connecticut, during the 1920s.

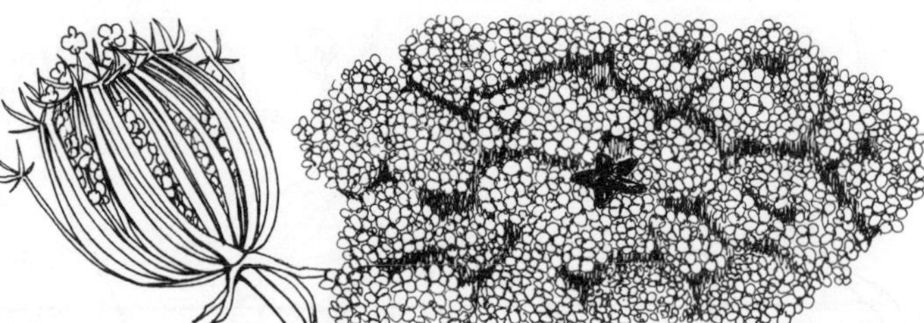

According to Carol Purcell (southern California), *"Flicking the inner part of Scotch broom releases a yellow powder. My sister and I used to 'take pictures' of one another by holding up a Scotch broom pod and sending up a puff of yellow."* (Author's note: Like flash powder?)

Horsetail (*Equisetum hyemale*), whose rough surface made it a good pot scrubber, suggested cigarettes to J. Stewart:

I would pick a stem and separate it into several cigarettes, preferring the tip end with the "ash." You could use the other segments also, and ask a playmate for a light. The naturally blackened end of each segment lent a further note of reality. We would poke these in our mouths, pretending to draw deeply and exhale. The chewed end had a fresh grassy taste, and the nicely pointed ash never fell onto anyone's carpet. (1940s)

Though the purple pokeberries were poisonous to eat, they could be crushed into a pulp that made gooey blood for becoming someone's blood brother (or sister). Some children used the juice for ink and wrote secret messages with a feather.

Sounds, Textures, Fragrances

In Alice Morse Earle's day, leaf-popping was a pastime of "noisy boys," who made a loud pop by placing broad leaves on the extended thumb and forefinger of one hand and striking them with the other. Earle had a disapproving

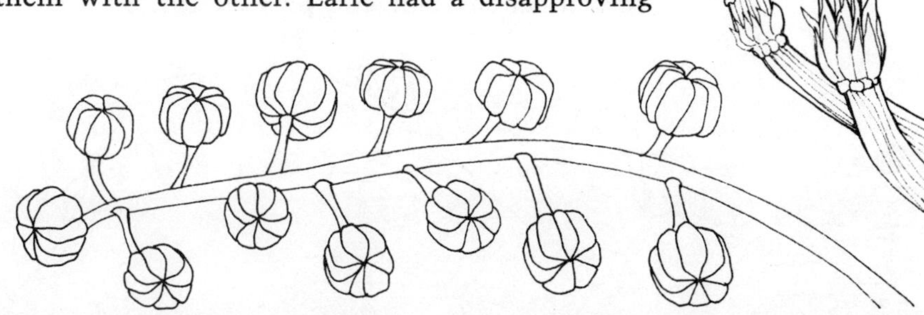

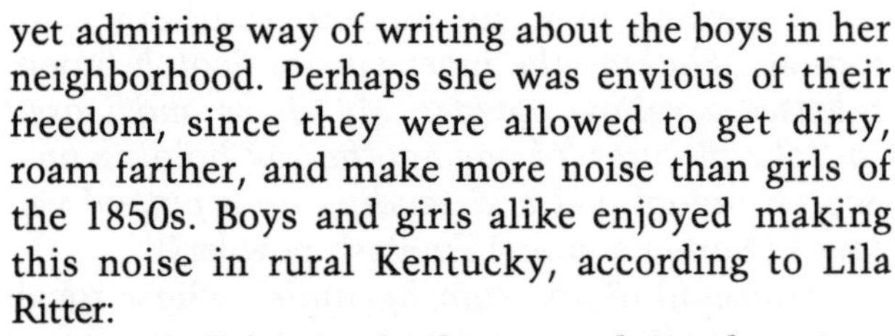

yet admiring way of writing about the boys in her neighborhood. Perhaps she was envious of their freedom, since they were allowed to get dirty, roam farther, and make more noise than girls of the 1850s. Boys and girls alike enjoyed making this noise in rural Kentucky, according to Lila Ritter:

We took big poplar leaves and put them over a hole made with forefinger and thumb and hit them with out other palm and made them pop. It was years before I realized that the name of the leaves was not "poppler," for the pop, but really was a tree called poplar. (1920s)

*"Bladder campions (*Silene cucubalus*) are miniature paper bags waiting to be burst,"* says J. Stewart. *"These little white roadside flowers produce a startlingly loud pop in proportion to their size. There's no need to blow them up — just pick a flower, squeeze the open end tightly shut with the thumb and forefinger of one hand, and tap it quickly against the back of your other hand."*

Stewart also recalls the texture of lily-pads: "Their undersides were coated with a gelatinous substance; I picked them just to feel their sliminess."

Growing up in North Carolina, where there were lots of pine trees, Robin Spear used to gather fresh pine needles and put them in old jars with tightly-closing lids. She says, "Opening these jars a few days or weeks later — I can still remember the pungent, piny freshness."

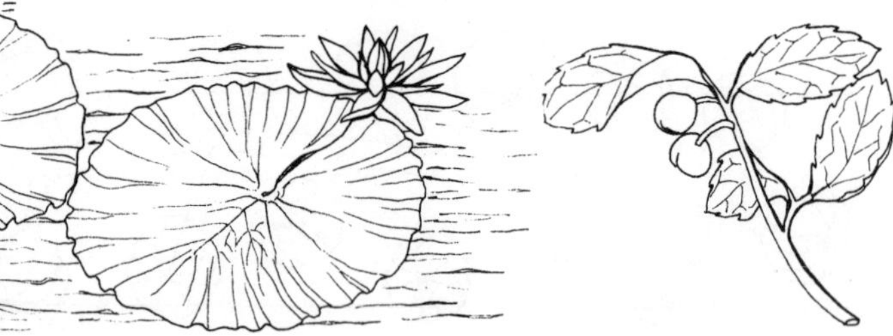

Hilda Badger Drummond broke off the dark green, glossy leaves of wintergreen (checkermint, checkerberry, teaberry) to sniff and taste.

Tastes

The tastes of wild plants, both sour and sweet, registered the strongest impressions. Alice Morse Earle's list of remembered tastes includes:

. . . rose-leaves and grass roots and smarting peppergrass. The sorrel and oxalis (which we called ladies' sorrel) and the curling tendrils of grape-vines gave an acid zest to our childish nibblings and browsings.

Frances Lehde (Kentucky, 1920s) also recalls the oxalis:

We loved to nibble the blossom buds and tender leaves for their tart taste. We called this wild oxalis with yellow blossoms sheep's shears or sour grass.

Other children ate this plant and called it pickles; anise they called licorice. Bob Burrell finds that he still pulls grasses to chew (usually timothy), a practice he began as a child. Sassafras twigs, according to Lila Ritter, "cleaned the mouth and sweetened the breath." Alice Betz remarks, "*In the center of the palmetto plant is a frond that has yet to unfold. When it is pulled from the plant, the tender broken end has a cabbage taste.* (Lakeland, Florida.)

Another treat that children discovered was the tender nutlet inside each sweet-fern bur. Af-

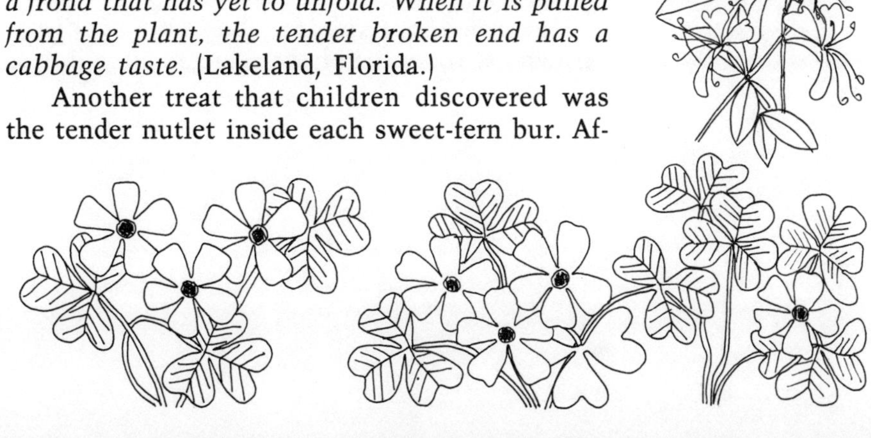

ter digging out a few of these morsels, one's fingers were stained a bright yellow, but that was a small price to pay for the delicacy.

According to Asa Gray, the sickly sweet fruit of the May-apple was consumed only by "pigs and boys," but some mothers made it into jelly or marmalade.

Clover heads were sweet, but the most mellifluous nectar was that of the honeysuckle. Alice Morse Earle mentions the coral honeysuckle (*Lonicera sempervivens*), but most would agree that, for sipping, *Lonicera japonica* 'Halliana' has no peer. Methods of sipping honeysuckle vary — from simply breaking off the stem end to Allen Lacy's precise directions:

Pinch off the green receptacle and ovary at the base of the long, trumpet-shaped flower, grasp the bottom of the pistil firmly between thumb and forefinger, and slowly pull it down through the tubular blossom until it emerges with a tiny, glistening drop of clear nectar to sip. And then another blossom and another, each giving its perfume to the tip of the tongue. A child with a sufficient store of fresh honeysuckle blossoms becomes kin to the gods who feed on ambrosia, kin to the bee, the hummingbird and the moth, to all the creatures of the air who pay their visits to this sweetest of all "serious weeds."

Even without sipping, children — and some grownups too — find the mere scent of honey-

suckle enough to make them happy, to glow with a sense of well being and of belonging to the world. It's even better when it mingles with other delicious odors of summer, with the scents of melting road tar, of new-mown grass, of mimosa trees nearby, of dusty roads after a sudden and brief shower of rain.

. . . I'm not even sure that anyone ever taught me this magic. I simply remember being three years old and standing by a dilapidated wooden fence covered with vines as I stole honeysuckle nectar drop by tiny drop from a handful of blossoms.

Anne K. Osia sipped her fill of nectar from honeysuckle, then put a supply of the flowers into a paper bag. During her travels she could stop to refresh herself with a sip or two.

Time has not diminished the appeal of honeysuckle, as Sally Getty can attest. She relates a trip to the zoo with a crew of kids in the summer of 1986:

The children were, naturally, impressed with the animals, but what made their day was the discovery of a giant honeysuckle bush. None of them had ever sipped the nectar of those lovely flowers, and upon learning their secret, they announced they intended to spend the rest of the day there. (Imagine a drop from the honeysuckle being more treasured than the sight of a Bengal tiger!)

Private Places

The time came for many children when they wanted to find a place to be alone with their thoughts and dreams. Each sought a secret spot that would be his or hers alone. Rose-Marie Vassallo-Villaneau remembers her hideout:

*There was a high pine tree (*Pinus sylvestris*) where I climbed with books to do my homework. The lowest branches were out of reach, so I had to throw a rope and perform acrobatics to haul myself up there, but after that the branches formed a ladder. My Latin and Greek dictionaries had a great fall from time to time, my favorite perching branch being more than thirty feet high; I can't say that the books were the better for that . . . or that my parents approved. Yet I felt so happy up there, so very much at home, that I did my work lightheartedly. I still remember the strong smell of resin (its stickiness too), the satiny touch of the bark in the highest part of the tree, and the wind brushing upon me and rocking my tree.*

J. Stewart recalls a number of beloved haunts from a childhood in Great Barrington, Massachusetts:

The cemetery, a shortcut on the way home from school, was a flat place, raised above the surrounding swamp lands. Beyond the grass-covered and tree-planted gravestone area, the cemetery's terrain was that of a dry steam bed — small pebbles and stones, flattened, rounded, tapered to a silky smoothness. Later in life, when

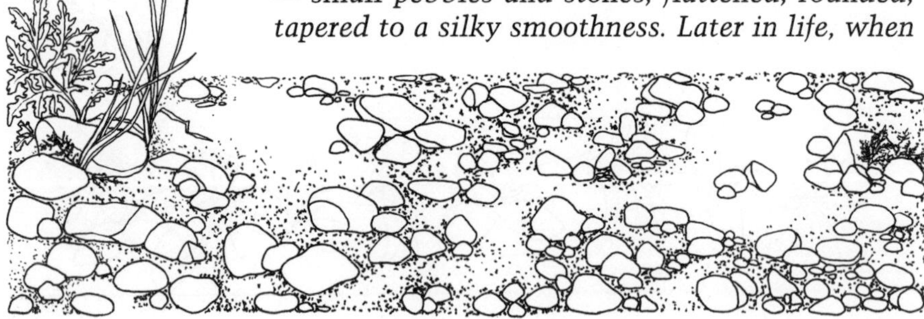

I became a rock gardener, I found that the term scree *described this pebbly open place. The vegetation was that of a scree — flat, silvery-leaved, economical plants spreading slowly outward more than upward. When the plants bloomed, the silver turned to waves of mauve, purple, and lavender.*

The swamp where I jumped from tussock to tussock was cheek-by-jowl to the cemetery but a study in contrasts. It was wet, thickety, filled with alders and pussy willows which closed in behind me a I advanced. Once inside, everything looked so much the same that, even though I knew I must be only a few feet from the road, I could become disoriented and a bit panicky as to how to get out. After a moment of heart-pounding consideration, a sound such as a car going by or a cow mooing would tell me which way was the road or which was the meadow, either of them a way out of the hemmed-in swamp. (Why did I continue going into the swamp, if it was a fearful place? Perhaps it was akin to hearing a bedtime story about scary creatures, while knowing that after it is over you are safe in your own bed.)

A favorite walk, and the closest to home, was through the woods, past a spring and brook; I dipped briefly into a meadow, scratched over or under a barbed wire fence, and then climbed up, up into a rocky upland pasture with a view of the valley below and the hills just beyond. There I would sit for a while, savoring the stillness.

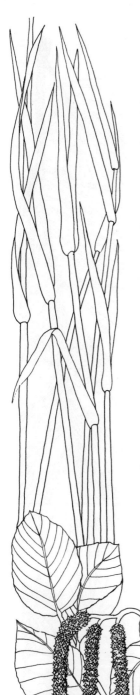

Bob Burrell found his own place near his home in Ohio:

In dense stands of brambles and blackberries I found a rabbit warren where a kid could carefully crawl through a maze of tunnels without being seen. One felt perfectly safe from imaginary bad guys, and one had a feeling that no one else knew about this very special, safe place. . . .

I used to think this was a personal aberration until I ran into a passage in the late Sigurd Olson's book, Open Horizons. *In [one] chapter, "The Pipes of Pan," he describes more eloquently than I that same kind of childhood experience. Olson allows you to once again enter a child's head and see things as the child does.*

The passage from Olson is this:

The Pipes of Pan sound early before the sense of wonder is dulled . . . I heard their music in many places as a child, but one of the best was an alder thicket where I used to hide, a veritable jungle that had never been cleared. The swamp began just beyond the garden fence, and I went there often, burrowing my way through the maze into its very center. There I had fashioned a nest on a dry little shelf. It was cozy and warm, and like any hidden creature I lay there listening and watching. Rabbit runways ran through it, and birds sang in the branches around me. Around the edge was a fringe of tall grasses, but the ground itself was cushioned with sphagnum moss, and little pools lay around me like jewels. During the summer, even at midday it was dark under the alders. In the fall, when the grasses were sere and the sun shone, those pools were flecked with blue and gold.

No great thoughts, revelations or new wisdom came to me, but something happened that I did not realize until long afterward; I became part of all the beauty, the tiny sounds, and everything around me.

The alder swamp was my refuge and no one came there but me. Only Mother knew and she understood it was mine and mine alone.

Alice Betz also understands about private places. She says, "*Now we have grandchildren. I know that leaving them alone to dream and to play is my part now.*"

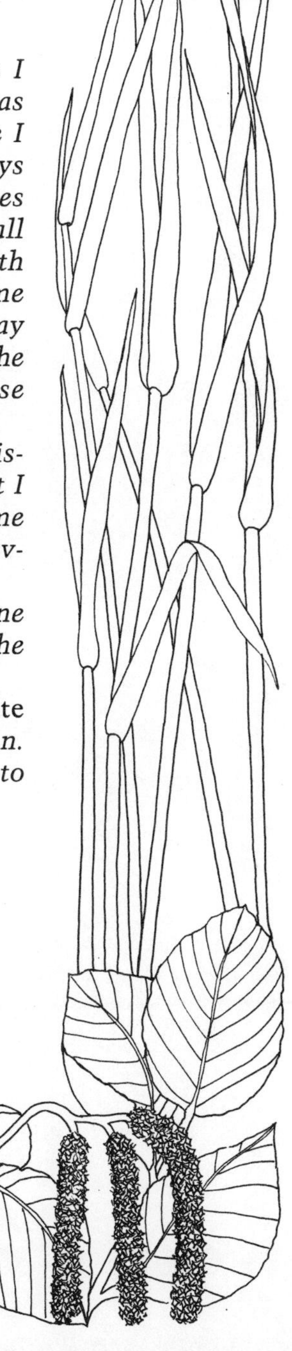

AUTUMN AND WINTER

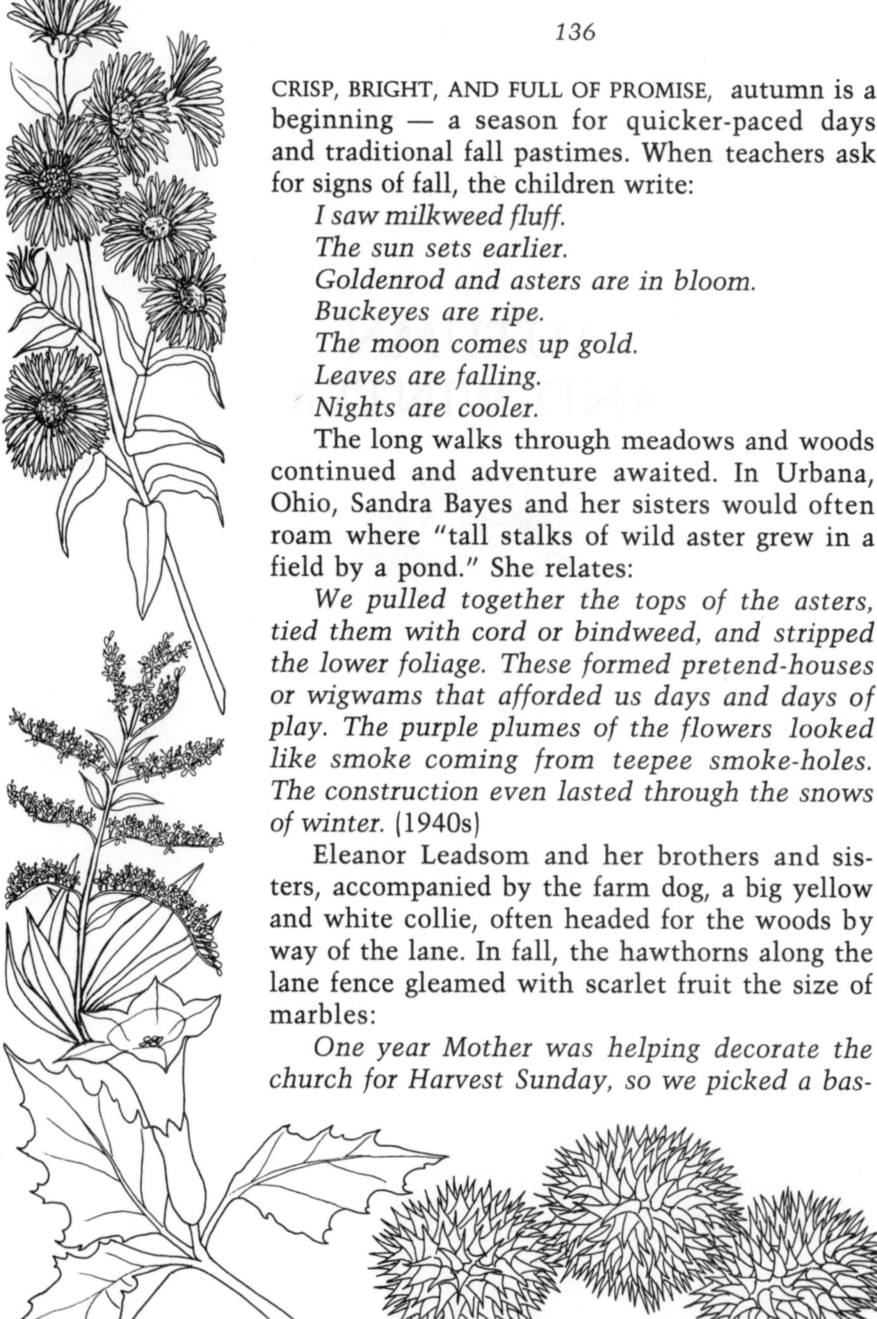

CRISP, BRIGHT, AND FULL OF PROMISE, autumn is a beginning — a season for quicker-paced days and traditional fall pastimes. When teachers ask for signs of fall, the children write:

I saw milkweed fluff.
The sun sets earlier.
Goldenrod and asters are in bloom.
Buckeyes are ripe.
The moon comes up gold.
Leaves are falling.
Nights are cooler.

The long walks through meadows and woods continued and adventure awaited. In Urbana, Ohio, Sandra Bayes and her sisters would often roam where "tall stalks of wild aster grew in a field by a pond." She relates:

We pulled together the tops of the asters, tied them with cord or bindweed, and stripped the lower foliage. These formed pretend-houses or wigwams that afforded us days and days of play. The purple plumes of the flowers looked like smoke coming from teepee smoke-holes. The construction even lasted through the snows of winter. (1940s)

Eleanor Leadsom and her brothers and sisters, accompanied by the farm dog, a big yellow and white collie, often headed for the woods by way of the lane. In fall, the hawthorns along the lane fence gleamed with scarlet fruit the size of marbles:

One year Mother was helping decorate the church for Harvest Sunday, so we picked a bas-

ket of the thorn apples, and with a needle and long strings of various lengths, we strung them into ropes, or chains. Mother looped the chains along the edges of a table filled with fruit and vegetables, and laid some of the shorter chains across the top — lovely to see, and we were so proud when people complimented her. She gave us full credit for the idea. Mother was like that.

There was a mystery that went unexplained for twenty years or more, a ritual attending the children's walks to the lane. Mrs. Leadsom recalls:

A very warty old log lay in the grass along the land fence. My little brother always ran past it with his arms thrust forward and his thumbs sticking out. Not until he was a grown man would he tell us why. It seems that he thought it was a crocodile sleeping there. He had heard that the only way to fight off a crocodile was to put its eyes out with your thumbs. He was ready!

On one of these walks the children were amazed to see a witch hazel tree that was covered with soft, feathery blooms. (Only later did they learn that autumn is the normal flowering time for *Hamamelis virginiana*). Henry David Thoreau admired the witch hazel, commenting in his journal, "*It is always pleasant to come upon it unexpectedly as you are threading the woods . . . Me thinks I attribute to it some elfish quality apart from its fame. I love to behold its gray speckled stems.*"

Along with its fall blooms, the witch hazel

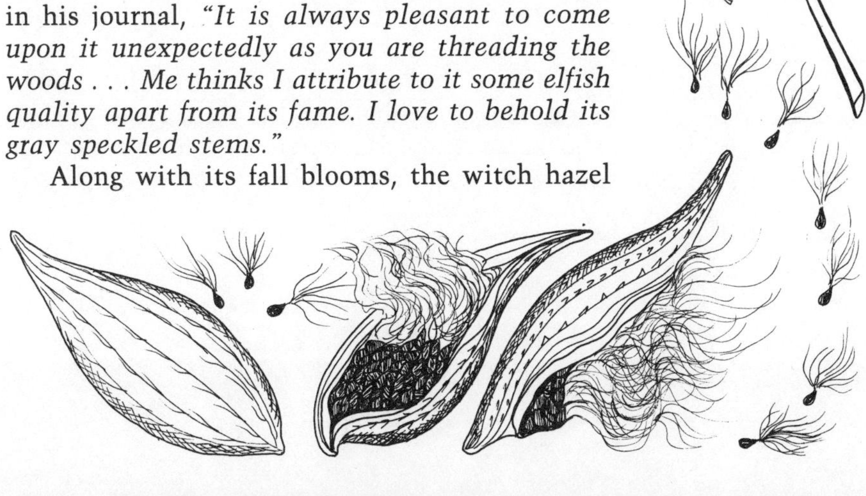

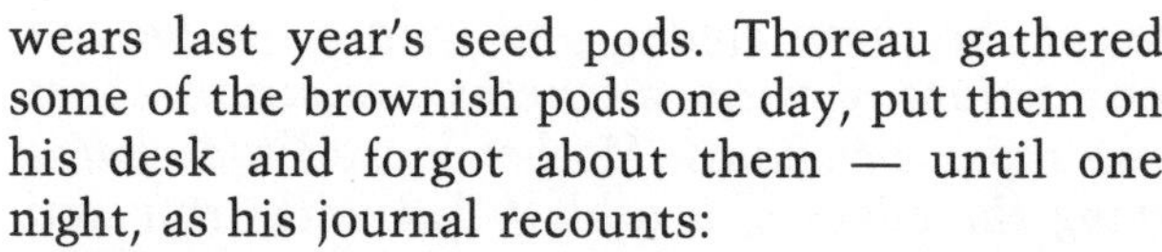

wears last year's seed pods. Thoreau gathered some of the brownish pods one day, put them on his desk and forgot about them — until one night, as his journal recounts:

Heard in the night a snapping sound, and the fall of some body on the floor from time to time. In the morning I found it was produced by the witch-hazel nuts on my desk springing open and casting their seeds quite across my chamber, hard and stony as these nuts were.[1]

In the autumn meadows canoe-shaped milkweed seed pods burst a side seam, releasing the fluffy seeds into the air. Each seed was said to be a "wish fairy." The custom was to catch a seed in flight, make a wish, and release it. If the seed flew off again, your wish would come true, but if the seed fell to the ground, your wish would not be granted.

J. Stewart remembers a more down-to-earth use for the milkweed silk:

In the 1940s we children were asked to help in the war effort by filling up bags of milkweed fluff. It was to be used as a stuffing for flotation vests in lieu of kapok, which grew in Japanese-controlled Malaya. We all imagined that someone would be rescued from the ocean wearing a vest filled with milkweed seed that we personally had picked.

Before the milkweed pods burst they could be opened up deliberately to extract the "fish." (The seeds and silk, when packed together in their pod, resembled a silvery-scaled carp.) Al-

ice Morse Earle molded "ingenious toys of the pith of the milkweed, which, when weighted with a tack, would always fall tack downward."

Autumn was the time to get sweet gum, which everybody liked to chew even though it could be nearly impossible to get unstuck from your teeth if it were not the right consistency. Many boys had a private sweet gum tree, the location of which was a jealously guarded secret. In the summer the boys tapped their tree (cut a hole through the bark where a branch joined the trunk) to let the gum ooze out. After the first autumn frost, it was time to harvest the gum. *"Every boy had his own hoard of gum,"* says Frances Lehde, *"but could usually be persuaded to give some away."*[2] (Kentucky, 1920s.) Jessie White attests to the popularity of the gum and adds, *"If you were lucky enough to get a big wad of this gum, you never thought of throwing it away. It had to be saved from one day to the next and was even shared with a favorite cousin or friend."* (Mississippi, 1930s.)

In the 1850s Alice Morse Earle and her friends took long autumn walks in the woods and gathered white birch bark, which they made into cornucopias and drinking cups, often cutting decorative designs into the bark. Chippewas traditionally made cones out of birch bark — tiny ones filled with hard (maple) sugar and hung on a baby's cradle board, and larger cones (also sugar-filled) for older children.

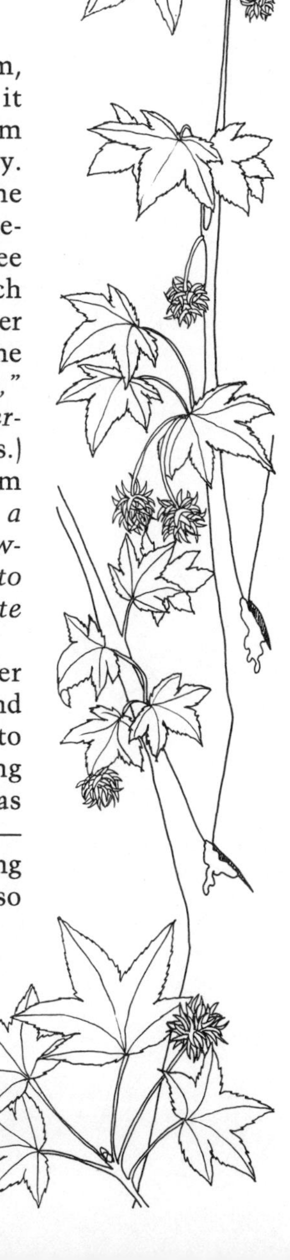

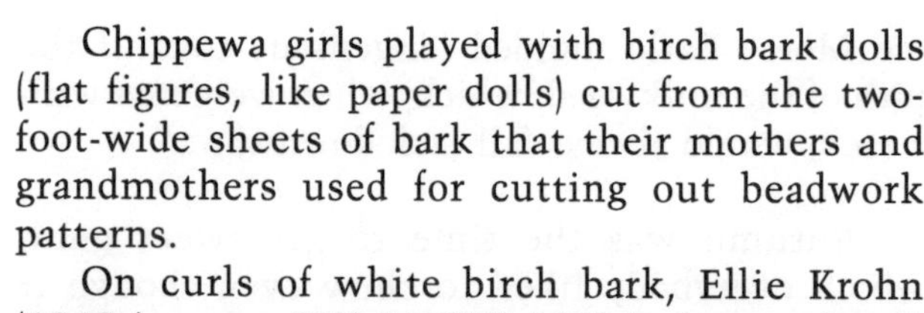

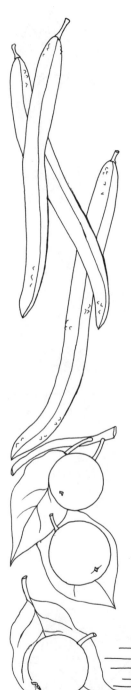

Chippewa girls played with birch bark dolls (flat figures, like paper dolls) cut from the two-foot-wide sheets of bark that their mothers and grandmothers used for cutting out beadwork patterns.

On curls of white birch bark, Ellie Krohn (1940s) wrote "EK LOVES LH" in hopes that L himself might find the note if he followed that same path through the Van Deusenville woods. (Massachusetts)

Bracket fungi, which grew in swirling shelves around the boles of trees, also presented a smooth white surface irresistable for writing on. With a pointed stick children would engrave drawings or cryptic messages, hoping to baffle others who came by later.

Jen Pekrul, of Canaan, Connecticut, found in her woods

. . .puffballs, some as big as footballs. What fun to kick these "devil's snuffboxes" and send out a puff of smoke! I don't think any of us kids knew at the time (1940s) that these so-called smokeballs were actually filled with millions of tiny mushroom spores that we were helping to sow.

Doll Tea Parties and Play Money

In autumn the tiniest dolls could have milkweed pod cradles with fluffy seed pillows and blankets. Larger dolls, propped up around the rock table, could dine on green beans (catalpa seed pods), scrambled eggs (goldenrod flowers),

and crab apples; they were served their tea in acorn cups and saucers. To make an acorn teacup, Lila Ritter's brother scooped out the inside of the nut, leaving the shell. After smoothing off the pointed end, he inserted a bent-twig handle and set the cup down into its acorn cap saucer. (Kentucky, 1920s.)

Alice Morse Earle used acorn cups and saucers in the 1860s but usually preferred more delicate tea sets, such as those made from rose hips. Little girls in the 1700s and 1800s took large rose hips (*Rosa rugosa*, for example, has fruits the size and color of cherry tomatoes) and fashioned miniature tea sets—teapot, sugar, and creamer—with bent pin handles. Earle describes finding one such rose hip tea set:

A few years ago I was present at the opening of an ancient chest which had not been thoroughly searched for years. In a tiny box within it was found some cherished belongings of a little girl who had died in the year 1794. Among them was one of these tea sets made of rose hips with handles of bent pins. Although shrunken and withered, the rose hips still possessed some life color, but they soon fell into dust. There was something most tender in the thought of the loving mother, who had herself been dead over half a century, who had thus preserved the childish work of her beloved daughter.

Playhouses could be swept with pine-needle brooms and decorated with colorful leaves. The medium of exchange and trade was the seed

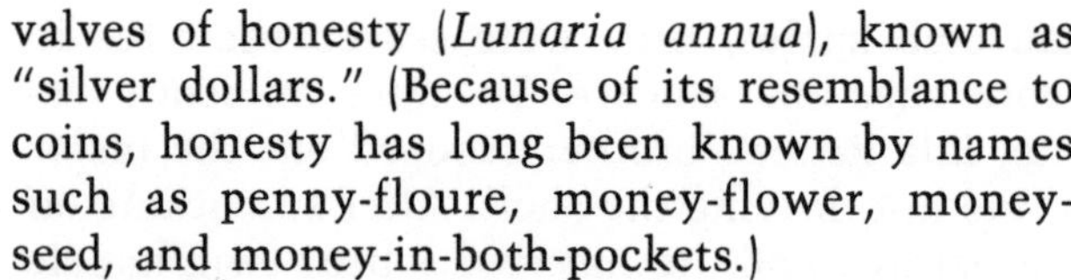

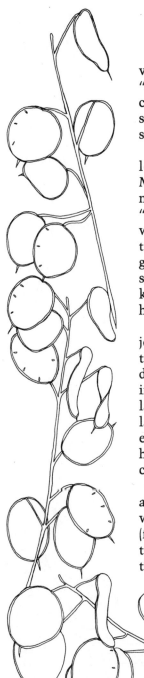

valves of honesty (*Lunaria annua*), known as "silver dollars." (Because of its resemblance to coins, honesty has long been known by names such as penny-floure, money-flower, money-seed, and money-in-both-pockets.)

There is a sad story about a man who collected these "silver dollars." In Worcester, Massachusetts, during the 1860s lived a man named Elmer. He was what people then called "feeble-minded" or "the village idiot"; nowdays we would say he had some form of mental retardation. Elmer slept in a deserted barn and gathered wild berries. He was also able to earn some money by weaving chair seats and baskets. The villagers gave him clothing and took him in when it was cold.

More like a child than an adult, Elmer often joined the children in their games. Together they picked the money plants for their "silver dollars." Unlike the children who were just making believe, Elmer thought that the "silver dollars" were equal to or more valuable than the large copper cents then in use. The storekeepers, who knew and understood Elmer, would give him a loaf of bread or a quart of molasses in exchange for the silvery seed valves.

One day, a couple of strangers walking along the road that led to the village met Elmer, who was gathering chestnuts. The two thieves (for that's what they were) talked to Elmer for a time, and were very interested when he mentioned his "hundreds and hundreds of dollars all safe for winter." The next three days were cold and rainy and Elmer did not appear, so his neighbors went to his barn, where they found that he had been beaten up. He had broken ribs and a high fever. His "silver dollars" were scattered all over the place. He got pneumonia and died a few days later.

The old barn fell down but all around it the next spring sprang up a vast meadow of money plant — lavender, purple, lilac, and white flowers. It was such a beautiful place that people drove in their carriages from miles around to see the flowers. And, of course, if you went there in the fall, you would find a meadow full of silver coins, dancing on their stalks, shining in the sunlight. (From Alice Morse Earle, *Old-Time Gardens.*)

Toys and Games

In the fall, the chinaberry trees gleamed with yellow missiles waiting to be shot out of an elderberry-stem popgun.[3] Annie Ohms Ericksen made these guns in the early 1900s when she was growing up on a farm near Harlan, Iowa. Her daughter, Mrs. Glenn Petersen, wrote down the directions:

[Take] a piece of elderberry stem. Push out the soft pith with a stiff wire and make a plunger out of a straight, smooth stick that fits snugly in the barrel.

To shoot the gun, you needed two berries or well-chewed paper wads (Annie used the latter):

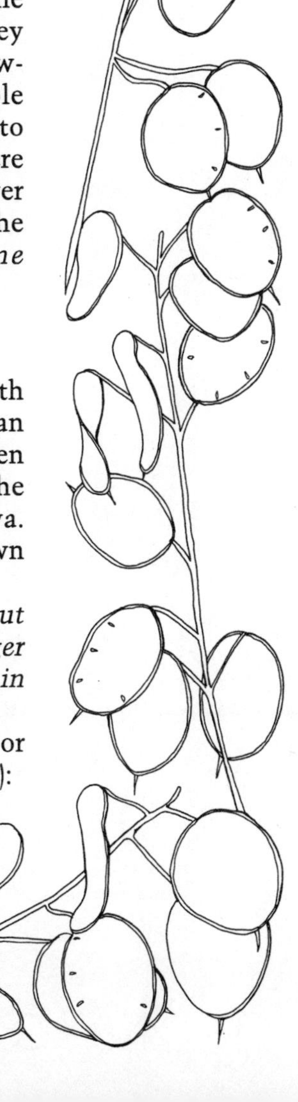

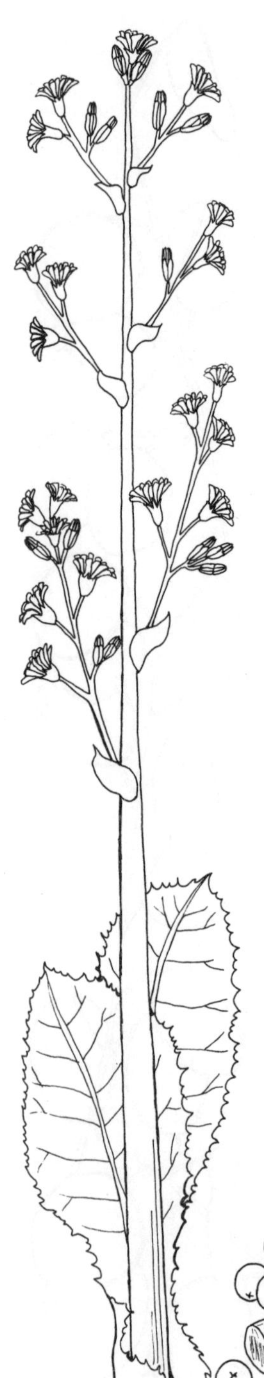

Push a paper wad almost through the tube and then a second one. Slam the plunger in and Pop! the first wad will shoot out.

Mrs. Ericksen explains that the popgun could be converted to a squirt gun:

Take a quarter-inch length of a small tree branch, put a pinhole in the middle, and plug up the end of the gun barrel. Fill the barrel with water, push the plunger, and now a stream of water will shoot forth!

Blowguns were simpler to make — just a length of cane or stalk of wild lettuce[4] (or even a popgun minus the plunger). The missiles, such as peas or beans, had to fit snugly within the blowpipe. The end of the blowpipe was cupped tightly in both hands, then the shooter took a deep breath, put the gun to his lips, and blew with all his might. Some kids knew how to make the darts out of sticks, thread, and thistledown.

The white, candelabralike flowers of the horse chestnut (*Aesculus hippocastanum*) were always left unpicked in spring, in anticipation of the glossy fruit in fall. Children collected these nuts, and buckeyes (*Aesculus glabra*), for necklaces, earrings, and little baskets. In the 1960s, Nancee Brightman strung them together for dolls; this was a bit difficult, since some of the chestnuts had to have holes drilled in two directions.

Many kids collected horse chestnuts just to look at and touch. Boys in Alice Morse Earle's neighborhood collected horse chestnuts, and she wondered why:

With what eagerness and hard work do boys gather these pretty nuts; how they quarrel with one another over the possession of every one; how stingily they dole out a few to the girls who cannot climb the trees, and are not permitted to belabor the branches with clubs and stones for dislodgment of the treasures, as do their lordly brothers! How carefully the gathered store is laid away for winter, and not one thing ever done with one horse chestnut, until all feed a grand blaze in the open fireplace.

Not all the nuts ended up in the fire because, when the nuts are first picked, according to Earle, "*[some] are tied to the ends of strings, and two boys holding the stringed chestnuts play cob-nut.*" The game of Cob-Nut originated in England and was first played with hazelnuts. Boys would carry strings of nuts for contests. Competition usually took place in the crown of a hat or a circle drawn in the dirt. One boy would put a hazelnut down in the circle, and the challenge was given. A second boy would take aim and fling down one of his hazelnuts to try to break the first nut. Usually he had three tries; if successful, his winning hazelnut was then pitted against another nut.

When the horse chestnut was introduced into England, Cob-Nut began to be played with these larger, firmer nuts and evolved into a game called Conkers. First recorded in 1848, Conkers

was (and still is) enjoyed throughout England.[5] Although the game was brought to America, it never became widespread. In fact, Leon Tannenwald, who played Conkers in the Bronx during the 1920s, says, "I have spoken to many people, but none of them used the horse chestnuts in this way." Mr. Tannenwald describes how he and his friends played their game:

When the ripe horse chestnuts [fell] to the street, we would collect them. We put a hole through the center of the nut with a nail or icepick, then put a string through with a knot at one end. Then one fellow would hold it up while the other fellow hit or whacked it with another nut. We would take turns until one of the nuts broke. The victor nut would be one year old. Then we would play someone else, and the victorious nut would carry the years of the losing nut. The boys would try all methods to make the nut hard so that it could become victorious.

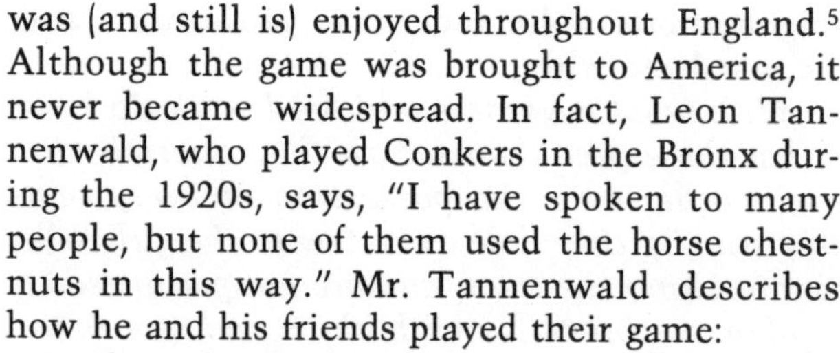

Two methods that English boys use to harden the nuts (recorded by Iona and Peter Opie in *Children's Games in Street and Playground*) are soaking them in vinegar or putting them in the oven for a while. Horse chestnuts saved for a year become very hard and somewhat shriveled; these "yearsies," in all fairness, should compete only against other "yearsies."

The English boys (Conkers is traditionally a boys' game, although girls sometimes play and are good at it) used the same method of scoring — one point for every victory. If a fifteen defeats

a ten, the winning conker is a twenty-six, and so on. Really spectacular conkers carry numbers in the hundreds before going down to defeat by another chestnut.

The American version (apparently) did not have a name and also lacked all the verbal lore of the original sport. In England there are ritualistic opening words, which vary from region to region. For example, in Yorkshire they say,

Ally, ally, onker,
My first conker.
Quack, quack,
My first smack. (Opie, 1969.)

If the strings get tangled, the players call out, "strings" or "tangles," and whoever cries out first gets an extra turn (or several).

Another game played with horse chestnuts is the following, again from the writings of Alice Morse Earle:

Two nuts are tied together by a yard of cord and by a catching knack, circled in opposite directions.

A native tree, the chinkapin (or chinquapin) yields fruits, similar to horse chestnuts, which are used in several games. Chinkapins (*Castanea pumila*) are native as far north as New Jersey, south to Florida, and west to Texas. In rural Georgia its fruit was used in the games Hull Gull[6] and Jack-Up-A-Bush (also called Jack-In-The-Bush.) In *Foxfire 3*, the Reverend Morgan recalls these games, both of which relied on

a handful of chinkapins. One person held a number of the nuts in his or her hand. A second person, the guesser, tried to guess how many nuts are held. For each one missed, the guesser has to give the first person a nut. If the guesser gets the number exactly right, the first person has to give the guesser all his chinkapins. The object was for one person to get all the nuts. Turns alternated. Both these games were played the same way, differing only in the set of words that opened the game.

HULL GULL
Person 1: Hull gull.
Person 2: How many?
Person 1: A handful.
(Person 2 takes a guess at the number.)

JACK-UP-A-BUSH
Person 1: Jack up a bush.
Person 2: Cut it down.
Person 1: How many licks?
(Person 2 then takes a guess, as in Hull Gull.)

Nuttiness

In the early 1920s the American chestnut (*Castanea dentata*) had not yet been wiped out by blight. Bill Johnson remembers these nuts as "the most delicious of all, boiled, roasted, and just raw off the trees." (Pennsylvania)

Carrying certain kinds of nuts in your pocket (or pocketbook) was said to be lucky. For example, buckeyes would prevent chills (Alabama), or

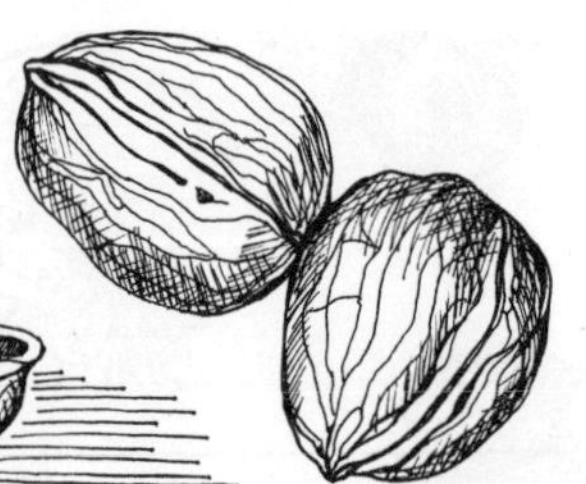

cramps (Ohio). The true chestnut, when carried, would keep rheumatism away (also said of the hickory nut). Carrying a horse chestnut would bring luck. *Lila Ritter remarks, "[Some] carried buckeye seeds in their pockets as good luck charms or maybe as a worry stone."* (Kentucky, 1920s.)

Little boys in Georgia carried rolls of hickory bark in their pockets, partly for good luck, but mostly as a commodity to trade for marbles or other desirable items. The boys would wet the bark, take it from the hickory tree, and peel it into little sections (some as narrow as strings), which they then wound into pocket-size rolls.

Children in parts of France observed this ritual: *"When you found twin nuts in a hazelnut or almond shell, you gave one to a friend, and ate the other yourself. The first one to say, "Philippine" to the other the next morning, won a gift.*[7] (Rose-Marie Vassallo-Villaneau, 1940s; Paul Sébillot, 1800s.)

When children think of walnuts and milkweed pods, they think of sailing ships.[8] Donna Brundage recalls:

I had two spinster aunts who were both kindergarten teachers with the patience of Job and more imagination than Albert Einstein. They would bake bread or cake using the whole walnut [meats] and then help me poke little sails made from construction paper in the empty shells. We owned an old farmhouse with a brook

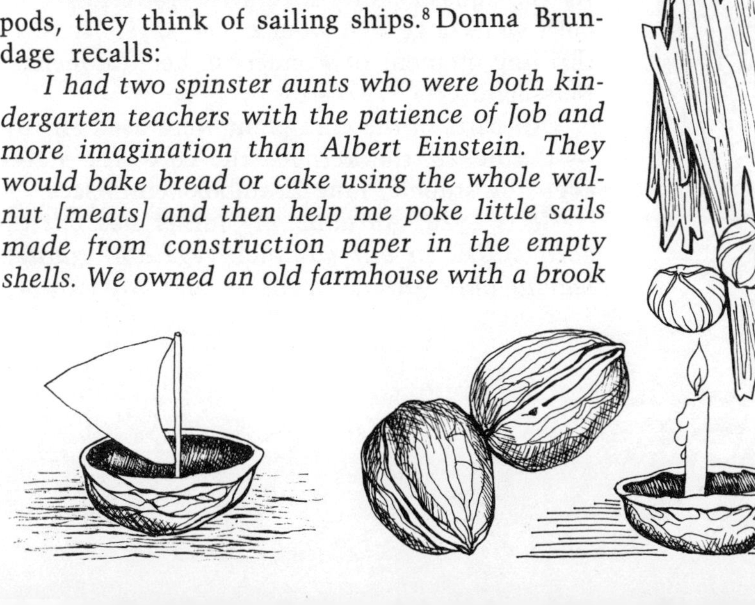

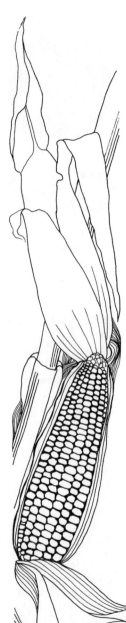

on the property . . . we'd drop our boats off one bridge upstream then run as fast as we could to watch them pass under the next bridge further downstream. (1950s, New York.)

Lizz Gilbert's mother helped her fill walnut shells with melted wax, and add a wick to make small candles (1960s). Georgeann Pierson combined boats and candles in a charming custom:

"We would melt the bottom of birthday candles so they would stick to our milkweed pod boats. After we lighted the candles we set our fairy boats adrift at twilight on the pond."

Squash and Corn

At home, the vegetable garden still held a few surprises. Three-year-old Grace Graham's father took her out to the garden one morning to find, *"a huge squash with my name on it . . . I couldn't imagine how the squash knew my name was Grace!"* Grace found out later that when the hubbard squash was very small her father had taken a nail and scratched her name on the rind. As the squash grew, so did the lettering, until both were large. No wonder she says, "It was a thrilling moment of wonder to me." (Stoneham, Massachusetts, 1920s.)

All parts of the corn plant were used for toys — the husks, the kernels, the cobs, the stalks, even the stubble. June Zsambok reminisces:

It is 1920. Autumn. My father has cut the corn stalks in our summer vegetable garden, leaving only stubble in the ground. My two best

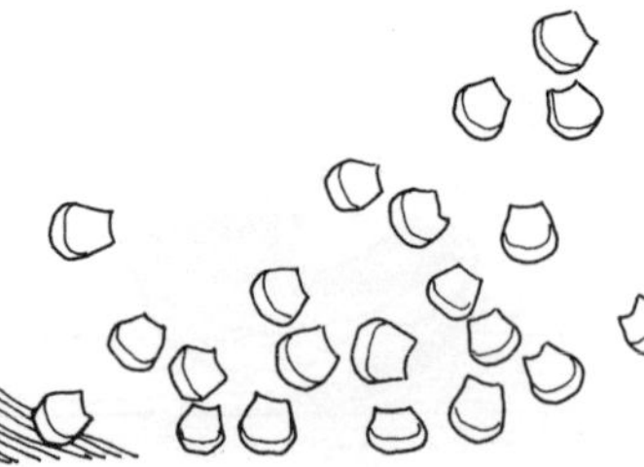

friends and I (all of us about eight or nine years old) have brought rag scraps and butcher-shop string pieces to the stubble area. We tear the rags, we cut the string. We drape and tie the rags onto the stubble, and voila! we have dolls. We have families walking to Sunday school, we have rows of children facing a school teacher, we have couples dancing. (I still remember the fun we had with those stubble dolls.)

Nancy Peiffer's grandfather made doll furniture for her and her cousins from the thin, straw-sized stems of corn plants:

He would cut or break the pieces to size and hold them together with straight pins. They resembled more a type of wicker than solid wood furniture. He built tables and chairs, benches and beds. (Pennsylvania, mid 1930s.)

If you could get hold of fresh corn kernels before they were used for food, you could, as Jan Ayers relates, *"press one over a front tooth and show everyone with a grin — gold tooth!"* (Greenville, Texas.)

To make a corncob doll, the first item needed was, of course, a corncob — freshly picked, husked, and scraped clean of kernels. A grown-up might have to help with the next step because a three-inch cut had to be made in the pointed end. (As the cut ends dried they would curve out a bit to form the doll's legs.) The cob then had to dry in the sun or inside in a dry, warm place. Fresh cornsilk could be glued on for the hair (blond to start with, but darkening to

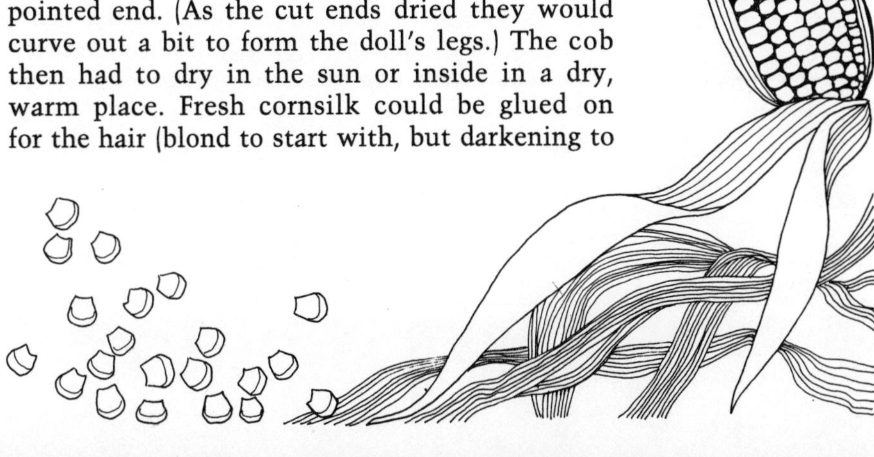

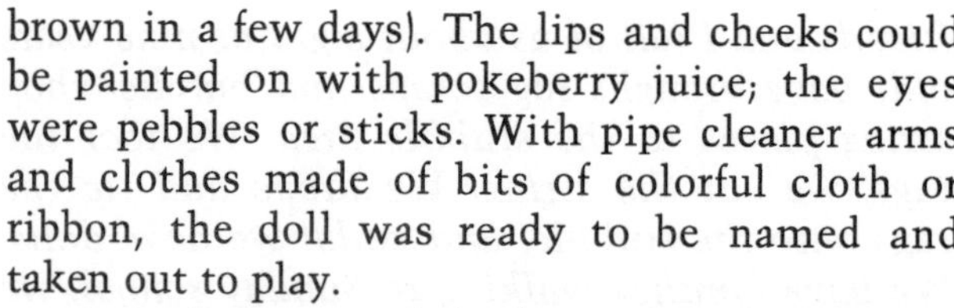

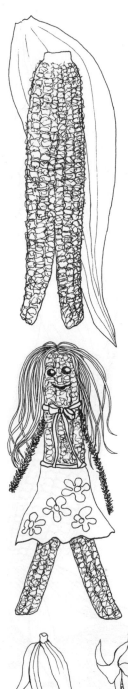

brown in a few days). The lips and cheeks could be painted on with pokeberry juice; the eyes were pebbles or sticks. With pipe cleaner arms and clothes made of bits of colorful cloth or ribbon, the doll was ready to be named and taken out to play.

A variation on this plain corncob doll was made by leaving the corn husk on the ear of corn. The girls pulled the husk up and out of the way so they could shell the corn and then put the ear to dry. When they were ready to make the doll, they soaked the husk in water to make it pliable. They put a wad of cotton batting or rags atop the broad end of the ear, pulled up a few husks over the stuffing, and tied them with string or yarn. This formed the head and hair; the damp husk ends sticking out above the stuffed head could be curled around a pencil to dry into ringlets. The girls painted a face on the husk head when it had dried. The remaining husks were cut into strips and braided for the arms and hands. More shucks, tied below the head, hung down for a long dress. (This cob-and-husk doll was sturdier than the dolls made from only the husks.)

Smoking

Dried cornsilk made a smoke that the more daring boys tried. The silk, Bill Johnson remembers, *"had the appearance of Five Brothers Smoking Tobacco, if not the taste — thank Heavens!"* (1920s, Pennsylvania). Bill adds that,

"The arrival of autumn also brought with it the dried catalpa seed pods, which with a little imagination could be used as cigars." Alice Morse Earle included on her list of "skillful and girl-envied accomplishments of boys" the making and smoking of pipes and cigars. She wrote of *"pipes of horse-chestnuts, corn cobs, or acorns, in which dried sweet fern could be smoked; sweet fern or grape-stem or corn-silk cigars."* (1860s)

In the 1940s girls were also smoking; Jenilu Richie recalls that she and friends in Memphis smoked grapevine:

We would break off pieces of vine (old growth or brown) about three inches long. We lit these with a match and puffed hard. They were only good for two or three puffs before they had to be re-lighted. The taste was so harsh we never inhaled.

Lila Ritter remarks, *"There was a plant growing in our woods that my brother used to roll up in Dad's cigarette papers and smoke; he called it "rabbit tobacco"* (Kentucky, 1930s). Rabbit tobacco (*Gnaphalium obtusifolium*, cudweed) grew in open woods and fields from Canada to the Gulf of Mexico. Its silver-gray leaves gave off a pungent lemony odor. Evelyn Vincent relates:

I'm sure Mama knew we smoked it, but she never let on. We rolled our smokes in pages from Sears catalog, and with no means of gluing the paper, except with spit, the cigarettes came

unrolled after a few draws. No matter. By then we were choking and wiping watering eyes. (Alabama, 1930s.)

Sherwood Moran, who grew up in Japan, remembers acorn pipes:

In the fall we could collect acorns, hollow out the tender inside, and stick an appropriately shaped twig in the side and think we were pretty sophisticated as we strutted around with pipes in our mouths. (Of course smoking was anathema in our missionary household.)

Apples

An apple bee (or apple cut, or apple paring) was a daylong social gathering filled with work and festivities connected with apples. Alice Morse Earle describes a typical nineteenth-century apple bee:

The cheerful kitchen of the farmhouse was set out with its entire array of empty pans, pails, tubs, and baskets. Heaped-up barrels of apples stood in the centre of the room. The many skillful hands of willing neighbors emptied the barrels, with sharp knives or an an occasional apple parer, filled the empty vessels with cleanly pared and quartered apples.

Sandra Bayes remembers similar days in Urbana, Ohio:

While Grandma, Mother, and assorted aunts made applesauce, jam, butter, pies, etc. they kept us from underfoot by giving us the rejected apples to fashion into apple doll heads. We

gouged and pinched facial features on them, propped them up on twigs (to form bodies to dress later) and stuck them on a cellar shelf, and forgot them. When we remembered we found they'd moulded or rotted. (Now I know and use the success recipe: soak the formed heads in lemon juice with a pinch of salt for preserving; check regularly while continuing to encourage feature distinction; insert cloves or beads for eyes before completely dry.) (1930s)

At Alice Earle's apple bee, the festivities went on into the evening:

When the work was finished, divinations with apple paring and apple seeds were tried, simple country games were played; occasionally there was a fiddler and a dance. An autumnal supper was served from the three zones of the farmhouse; nuts from the attic, apples from the pantry, and cider from the cellar. The apple quarters intended for drying were strung on homespun linen thread and hung out of doors on clear drying days. When thoroughly dried in sun and wind, these sliced apples were stored for the winter by being hung from rafter to rafter of various living rooms and remained thus for months (gathering vast accumulations of dust and germs for our blissfully ignorant and unsqueamish grandparents) until the early days of spring, when applesauce, apple butter, and the stores of apple bin and pit were exhausted and they then afforded, after proper baths and soakings, the wherewithal for . . . dried apple pie.

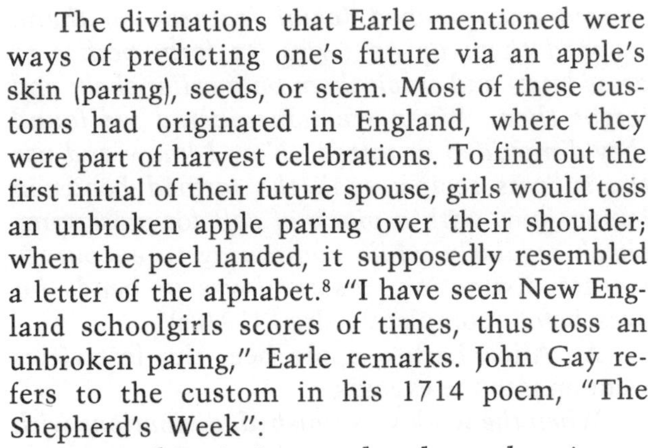

The divinations that Earle mentioned were ways of predicting one's future via an apple's skin (paring), seeds, or stem. Most of these customs had originated in England, where they were part of harvest celebrations. To find out the first initial of their future spouse, girls would toss an unbroken apple paring over their shoulder; when the peel landed, it supposedly resembled a letter of the alphabet.[8] "I have seen New England schoolgirls scores of times, thus toss an unbroken paring," Earle remarks. John Gay refers to the custom in his 1714 poem, "The Shepherd's Week":

I pare this pippin round and round again,
My shepherd's name to flourish on the plain,
I fling th' unbroken paring o'er my head
Upon the grass a perfect L *is read.*

Sandra Bayes and her sisters did this in the 1930s, in Ohio. Since they were not yet teenagers, she remarks, "We were oft married before we were out of puberty." Alice Betz, who grew up in south St. Louis, Missouri during the Depression, remembers that it was the *right* shoulder that the peel was thrown over and remarks that "the peel could be viewed from all angles to determine a desired initial." She also recalls a custom that followed immediately after the throwing of the peel: "*We counted the seeds inside to see how many children we'd have in later life.*" In Alice Earle's day, the girls named each of the apple seeds after a boy they liked, then moistened all the seeds and stuck them on their cheek or forehead. They chanted:

Pippin, pippin, paradise,
Tell me where my true love lies!

The seed that stayed in place the longest was your true love.[9]

Another kind of apple seed predicting was done while counting the seeds to the accompaniment of this rhyme:

One I love, two I loathe,
Three I cast away,
Four I love with all my heart,
Five I love, I say.
Six he loves me, seven he don't.
Eight he'll marry me, nine he won't.
Ten he would if he could, but he can't.
Eleven he comes, twelve he tarries,
Thirteen he's waiting, fourteen he marries.[10]

William Newell's version, from New England at the beginning of the nineteenth century, is similar except for the last two numbers. It ends:

Thirteen wishes, fourteen kisses,
All the rest little witches.

The apple stem also could make predictions. As a girl twisted the stem she would recite the alphabet until the stem snapped off. The letter she said at that moment was the first initial of her true love. (The letters at the beginning of the alphabet were favored because it never took many twists to pull off the stem.)

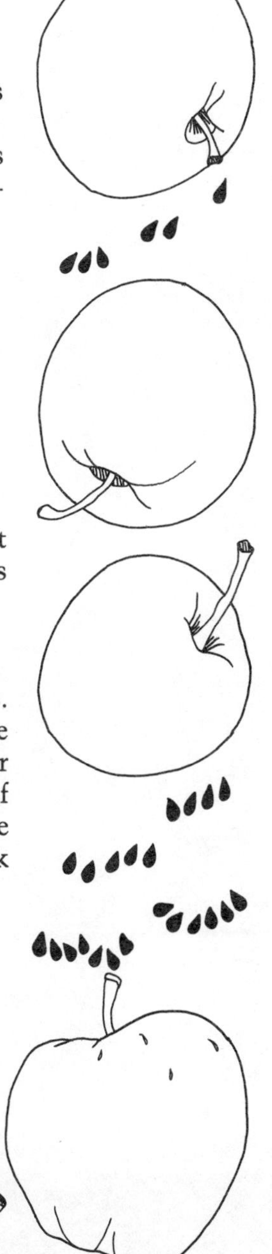

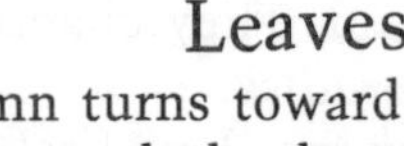

Leaves

As autumn turns toward winter the weather grows colder, and the leaves, having flaunted brilliant colors, fall to the ground and inspire a final fling! Helen Hooven Santmyer recalls:

In those last brief weeks or days before the rains came, and winter, and ruined the leaves, we gave up our other games after school to play in them. We heaped them up and ran and jumped in them or turned somersaults, or buried each other and were resurrected with leaf crumbs in our hair and mouths. We spread them out and raked them into lines, and each of us had a house after his own plan, with leaves for walls, and for floors the vivid green grass of late fall combed flat by the rake. (Xenia, Ohio early 1900s.)

Forty years later, in Charlotte, Illinois, the high-spirited leaf-play continued for Ann James van Hooser and her friends:

At our one-room school surrounded by huge trees, we children constructed gigantic forts of

leaves. I was always small for my age, but it seems to me that the walls of the forts may have been about eighteen inches high, sometimes more, since I remember the enemy leaping over the walls and vanishing from sight. We hid in the forts, venturing out occasionally with our toy guns and rifles to make raids on whichever group was the Indians. I was invariably an Indian, since Mennonite children were not allowed guns, but I could fashion a bow out of a branch and string. Our forts had many rooms: storerooms, secret rooms, and of course, the jail, which was easily broken out of. We girls hid in the fort with our baby dolls, which we always protected with our lives as the danger of their being kidnapped by the Indians was great. Strangely enough, on the days when I was an Indian, I kidnapped babies with great glee, riding up to the fort on my horse — a stick with a length of rope tied to the end . . . for a bridle.

When Ann was at home she constructed leaf houses:

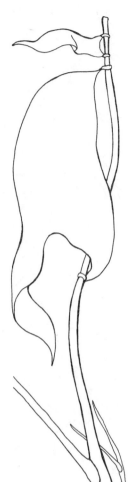

I made a bedroom for each of my baby dolls. I had a kitchen, living room, dining room, and especially a secret room. I would carry out blankets to spread in my own bedroom on a soft leaf pile. There were always secret runways and quick exits in case of attack. I remember my houses spreading across a wide area of lawn, ranging up to twenty feet.

In the 1960s in Bel Air, Maryland, Anne K. Osia's father, who was rector of the Episcopal church, "organized work parties for leaf removal in the church yards." There the huge piles waited until it was time for burning.

These piles became magnificent forts in which my brother and I made tunnels and shot stick arrows from stick bows. We conquered lands with stick swords and spears. Another game for the leaves was appropriately called Squirrels. It involved gathering acorns and hiding them from the other squirrels.

One fall, Alice Betz's father did extensive pruning of their trees and shrubs. As she remembers:

There was a huge pile of branches drying to burn later. That pile gave us girls hours of fantasy play. I recall it being a sailing ship, and we climbed the rigging and set sail for far-off places. Jumping up and down on certain branches made the whole ship shake from pounding waves as we battled storms. We braved pirate attacks on the open seas of our make-believe world. (St. Louis, Missouri, 1930s.)

Finally, the waiting leaves and branches were burned. Bonfires filled the air with hauntingly fragrant smoke. Earlier in the fall, Sandy Bayes and her sisters had gathered cattails from the nearby factory pond. After they had plunged them head-down into a pail of water, their grandpa hung the cattails upside down in the shed "to weather some." A few weeks later, when they were dry and stiff, their Dad dipped the cattail heads in kerosene. Each of the girls then had a torch to light from the bonfires. Sandra remembers: *"We whooped up Indian sum-*

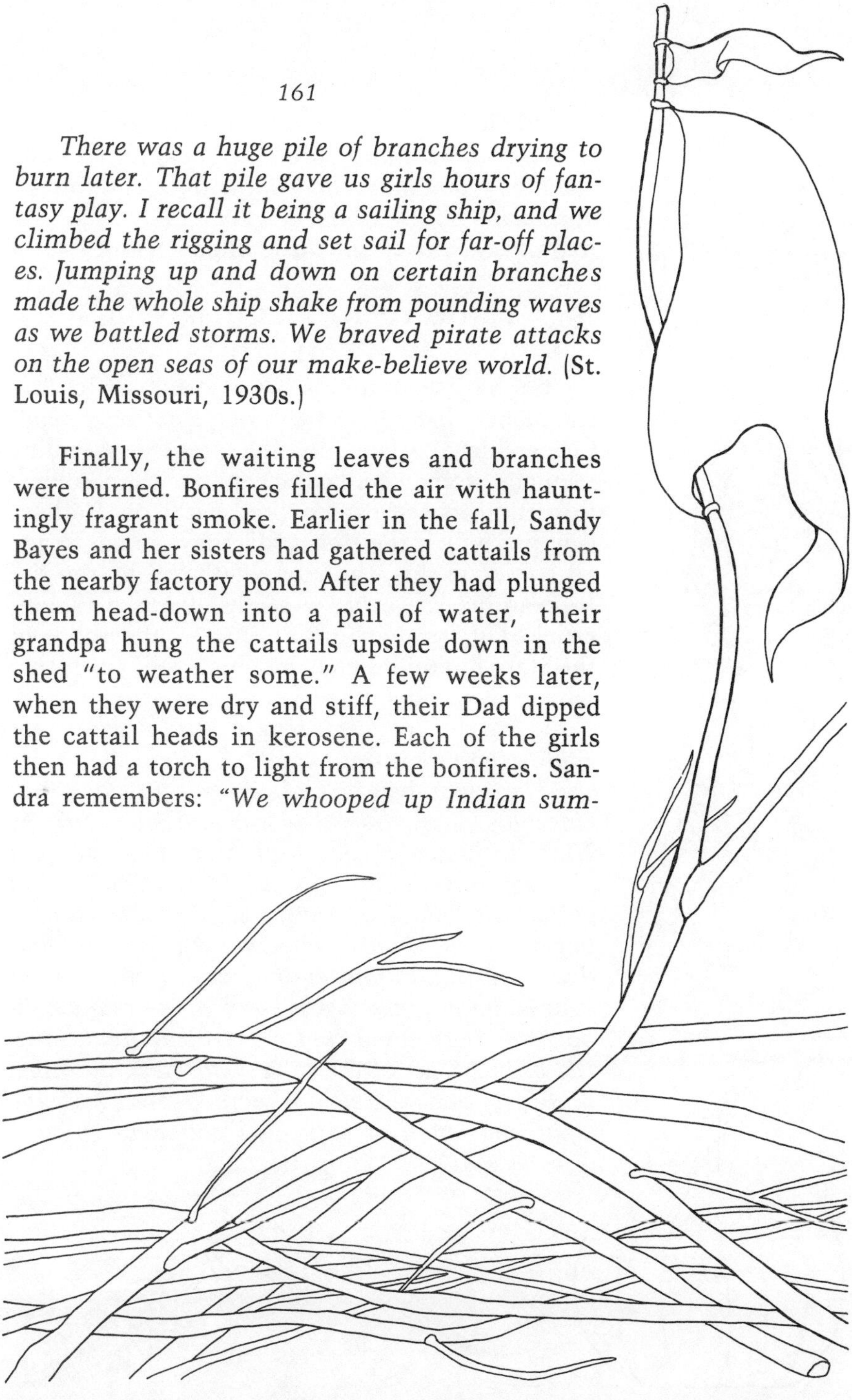

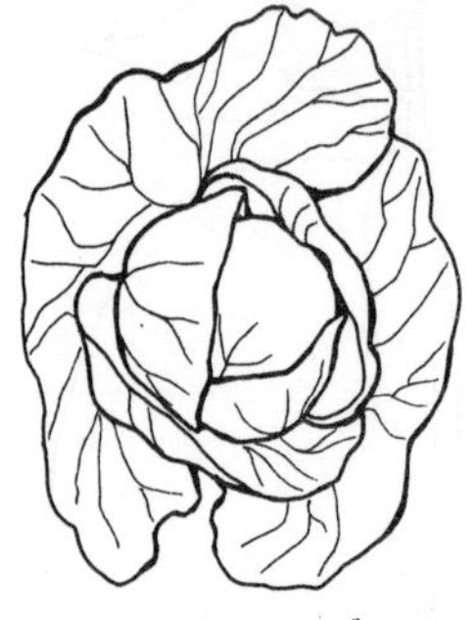

mer war dances and parades. Once, on Halloween night, Dad lined the walk with cattail torches and jack-o'-lanterns and lit them all at once. The fragrance, colors, and thrill linger." (1940s)

Halloween, Thanksgiving, and Christmas

Cabbage, pumpkins, corn, and apples are the plants that figure in the celebration of Halloween. In Scotland, in the late 1800s, young men and women walked one by one (blindfolded) into the cabbage garden (kail-yard) on Halloween and pulled the first stalk they found. When all had done this, the group gathered by the fire to examine the cabbage stalks. Large or small, crooked or straight, fat or thin — the shape of the stalk foretold the characteristics of the future wife or husband and led to much hilarity.[11]

J. Stewart recalls using cabbages for a pre-Halloween prank:

The night before Halloween in Great Barrington, Massachusetts, was called Cabbage Night in honor of the prank traditional to that evening. Boys (only boys, as I remember) would go out after dark on that night to look for cabbages. (In the 1940s the numerous Victory Gardens still had cabbages in them at the time of year.) The pranksters gathered up as many cabbages as they could find and rolled them down the hilly streets of the town. The next morning, motorists and pedestrians were greeted with the sight and smell of squashed cabbages. I seem

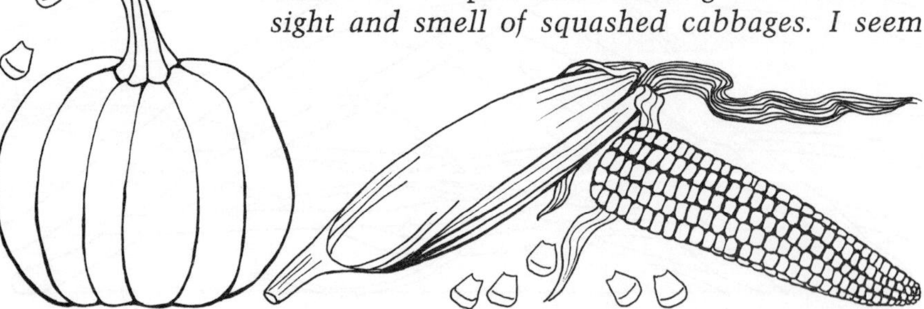

to recall that Cabbage Night went on for a number of years and then stopped. Perhaps cabbages fell into short supply after WWII. Either that or Police Chief McCarty grew less tolerant of the custom.

Halloween brings to mind candy corn, Indian corn, and (to Sandy Bayes) a mischievous use for the kernels:

Our Halloween noisemaker [and] trick-or-treat calling card was dried corn thrown onto porches. We carried the full cobs with us, shucking off handfuls of kernels as we walked along.

She goes on to describe other customs of Urbana, Ohio:

We also went equipped with half bars of Ivory soap or paraffin to soap windows where residents handing out no treats got the treatment! Of course, in a small town in the 1930s and '40s, people expected and anticipated such revelry. In the rural areas kids put up roadblocks of blazing cornstalks and up-ended outhouses. When vandalism was legitimized once a year, it was greatly eliminated the rest of the year.

In the United States, the pumpkin is the plant most closely associated with Halloween. Making jack-o'-lanterns is a custom of long standing; Alice Earle wrote of carving them in the 1850s:

A favorite manner of using the autumn store of pumpkins was in the manufacture of Jack o'

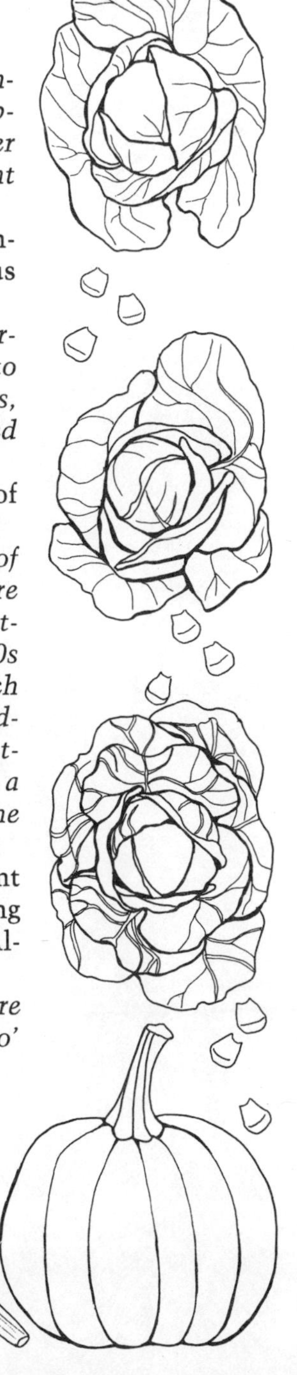

lanterns, which were most effective and hideous when lighted from within.

In parts of England children celebrate Punkie Night by carving elaborate jack-o'-lanterns from mangel-wurzel (a large yellow beet). The beets are first hollowed out, and in the half-inch shell of flesh remaining are carved flowers, animals, houses, even whole scenes.

To decorate the Thanksgiving table, children made creatures such as milkweed pod lovebirds, thistle porcupines, pine cone animals, and apple seed mice with thread tails and tiny paper ears. With pine needle dolls dancing on a mirror, you could have a whole skating party. Alice Morse Earle made these dolls:

A thickly growing cluster of needles was called a lady. When her petticoats were carefully trimmed, she could be placed upright on a sheet of paper, and by softly blowing upon it could be made to dance.

Chippewa children made their pine needle dolls from the red pine (Norway pine, *Pinus resinosa*), which had long needles. They cut across the needles, leaving shorter lengths for the arms and evening off the hem of the skirt. To make the dolls dance, they put them on a piece of birch bark or tin and jiggled it skillfully. (Minnesota, early 1900s.)

Cones from the pitch pine (*Pinus rigida*) delighted Alice Earle in two ways:

A winter's amusement was furnished by

gathering and storing the pitch pine cones and hearing them snap open in the house. The cones could also be planted with grass seeds and formed a cheerful green growing ornament.

During the holiday season there would often be a houseful of company. A favorite aunt might show her nieces and nephews the bearded Santa in every peanut and how the peanut shells made dancing shoes for your fingers. A mischievous cousin, seeing the holly decorations, might dare someone to, "Take hold of this leaf," proclaiming, "Look, it doesn't prick," while grasping a leaf. (The secret was the same as the nettle challenge — if you were timid and touched the holly leaf gingerly, it *would* prick, but if you grabbed it boldly, it would not hurt you.)[12]

During the long winter evenings, boys could practice whittling. From the age of three or four country boys carried pocket knives and used them for work and play. Alice Earle lists projects — carving heads for "old-women dolls of hickory nuts," and "making baskets and brooches by cutting or filing the furrowed butternut or the stone of a peach; also fairy baskets, Japanesque in workmanship, of cherry stones." Hilda Badger Drummond's father carved her peach baskets when she was five (in 1918):

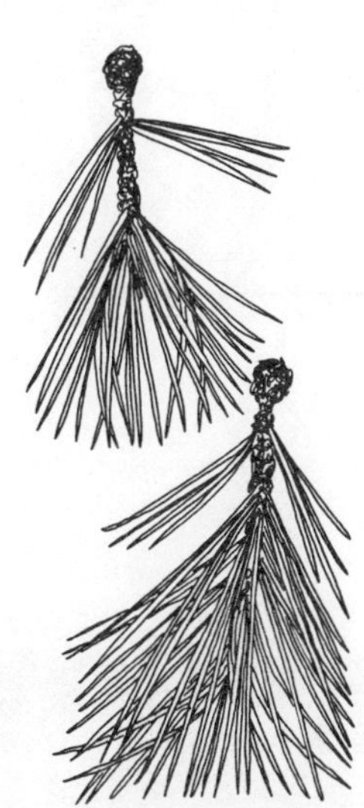

He would shellac them to make them shiny, and we would proudly hang them on a ribbon around our necks. Of course we thought we were pretty special and our father was the smartest.

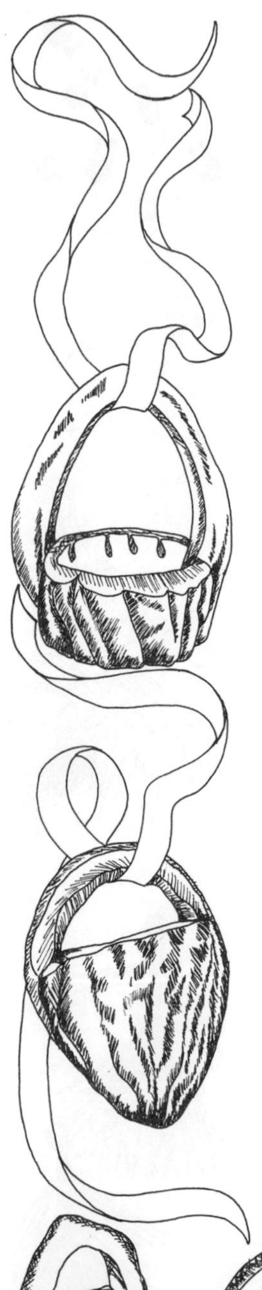

That same father carved tiny baskets out of cherry stones as well. I still have, among my treasures, one of his cherry stone baskets and a peach seed basket.

And from Millie Bostrom (Montana, 1920s):

When I was very small, my big brother would carve little baskets from peach seeds. Almost ten years ago my brother retired, and I sent him a card with the message, "Best wishes and a happy retirement to my big brother, who could carve the nicest peach seed baskets a little girl could ever have." He had forgotten all about it, but started carving again and didn't quit until he'd carved one for [each of] his daughters, granddaughters, and yes, even two for me. I treasure mine and will pass them on to a niece, who wants them for her children.

One Christmas Anne Osia arranged a special surprise. She had saved milkweed fluff from earlier in the fall, and when she wrapped the packages she put some "fuzzies" in each one, on top of the gift. When her friends and family opened their presents, "fuzzies" flew all over the place. (Not everyone enjoyed the surprise.)

Stories

Winter was storytelling time. In the 1930s on a winter evening in Oklahoma, the Spradlin kids would try to persuade Dad (Clarence) to recite his tale about pawpaws and other things beginning with *p*. Harold Spradlin remarks, "Dad

would blow air out of tightly clasped lips on every *p* in this story."

One day I saw a possum in a pawpaw patch pickin' up pawpaws and puttin' 'em in his pocket to make a pawpaw pie. I went fishing and caught a perch, a pike, and a pickerel. I made a pie out of the perch, a puddin' out of the pike, and gave the pickerel to the pup. It made the pup sick, and he puked . . . and puked . . . and puked.

"Lord knows there wasn't a hell of a lot to laugh about in Oklahoma in the heart of the dust bowl during the Great Depression," recalls Mr. Spradlin, "but laugh we did!"

Grace Graham never tired of the following story, told to her in the 1920s:

There was a little boy who was bored because he had nothing to do. He kept pestering his mother, asking, "What can I do now?" His mother soon tired of this and told him to go look for something round, red on the outside, white on the inside, and having a star in the middle.

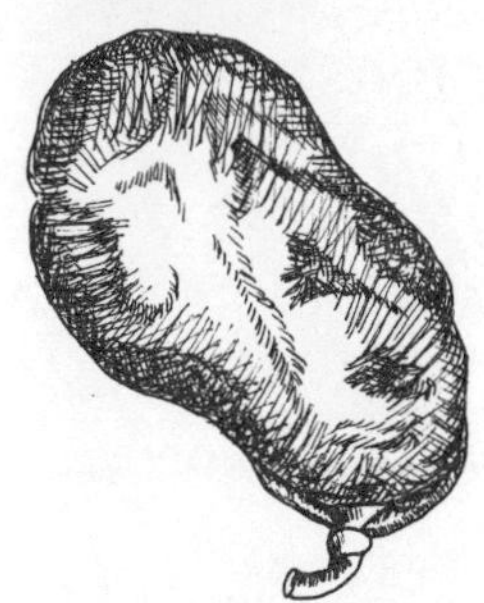

He walked and walked, stopping at all the farms nearby asking everyone if they knew of something red on the outside, white on the inside, with a star in the middle. No one could help him, and he soon grew very tired and sat down under a tree to rest.

As he lay dozing, a nice red apple fell out of the tree right next to him. By this time he was very hungry, and he took out his pocket knife

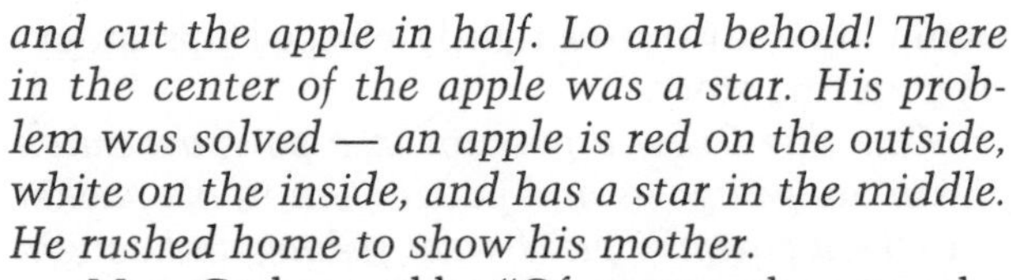

and cut the apple in half. Lo and behold! There in the center of the apple was a star. His problem was solved — an apple is red on the outside, white on the inside, and has a star in the middle. He rushed home to show his mother.

Mrs. Graham adds, "Of course, the one who tells this story should have an apple at hand to show. The star appears when the apple is cut in half crossways (at right angles to the stem)."

Outdoors in Winter

Winter as well as summer gave us many happy garden hours. Sometimes a sudden thaw of heavy snow and an equally quick frost formed a miniature pond for sheltered skating at the lower end of the garden. A frozen crust of snow (which our winters nowadays seldom afford) gave other joys. And the delights of making a snow man, or a snow fort, even of rolling great globes of snow, were infinite and varied. More subtle was the charm of shaping certain things from dried twigs and evergreen sprigs, and pouring water over them to freeze into a beautiful resemblance of the original form. These might be the ornate initials or name of a dear friend, or a tiny tower or pagoda. I once had a real winter garden in miniature set in twigs of cedar and spruce, and frozen into a fairy garden. (Alice Morse Earle, 1860s.)

Winter brought frost pictures on the window panes — ferns, flowers, and leaves more exotic than those seen in the summer — and six-foot long icicles to bring inside and put in the bathtub. Not to mention the joys of navigating the hills on a jack-jumper,[13] making angels in the snow, and trying to see who could identify the most animal tracks.

At least once a winter, a storm would leave a crystalline legacy: every plant from tiniest moss to towering beeches would be encased in spun glass, iridescent in the bright sun that so often follows an ice storm.

One February night in a small Connecticut town, a windstorm broke branches off the Norway maples. Sap oozed out of every break and froze into maple icicles.[14] Early the next morning a few children joyfully plucked this rare treat. They let the ice dissolve on their tongues, savoring its cold, mapley sweetness. The icicles melted away by noon, but were never forgotten by those who had tasted them. In memory the icicles became even sweeter, part of a store of such moments that nourish and sustain icicle- and honeysuckle-sippers throughout their lives.

Puzzlements

I am baffled by some of the bits of plant lore I turned up during my researches, and I hope that readers can help clear up the mysteries. Please write to me about these questions — or about any other plant lore recollections you'd like to share (for a hoped-for second volume of *Honeysuckle Sipping*).

Jeanné Chesanow
c/o Down East Books
P.O. Box 679
Camden, ME 04843

1. Has anyone eaten the *oak apples* (honeysuckle apples, galls)? Can you describe the texture and taste and tell when to eat them?
2. *Plantain duels.* I can't find anyone in the United States who dueled with plantains, that venerable game described in the Introduction.
3. What is the *snakegrass* that Alice Morse Earle mentions? (It looks like a parasol.)
4. What seed pods look like (a) *tongs* or (b) *a hoop-skirt*?

5. *Jack in the Pulpit.* I have not been able to make Jack "preach." I have pinched many plants at the base of the spathe and nary a squeak! What is the secret?
6. *How do you make a compass out of oat grass?* The awns lean to left or right, predicting rain or fair weather. (Colette wrote about these; her mother often made them.)
7. *The rose hip tea set*: I can imagine what it looked like, but would like to see a photograph of one or hear from someone who has made or seen such a set.
8. *The ship made of iris leaves.* Despite a photograph of one in Alice Morse Earle's book, I cannot figure out how to make the intricate folds and insertions to create this graceful craft.
9. *A braided cat ladder* is also mentioned by Alice Morse Earle. It too is made by folding iris leaves, but how?
10. *Ducks made of cattail leaves.* Pictures in Densmore are clear, but for the novice not sufficient. I need step-by-step instructions.
11. *Thistle dolls.* I tried these, but got only sore fingers and no "skirted dancers."
12. *Cornstalk witches.* Mentioned by Alice Morse Earle. Are these dolls, but made from stalks instead of cobs or husks?
13. Manasseh Cutler, writing in 1786, says: "I was pleased with a number of perfectly

white silken balls, suspended by small threads along the frame of the looking-glass. They were made by taking off the calyx of the thistle at an early stage of blooming." (*Child Life in Colonial Days,* pp. 392-393). Please send me some of these in a little box and tell me how you made them.

14. *Poppy shows*. I'd like stories about, accounts of, and pictures of these.
15. *Cornstalk fiddles and birch bark squawkers.* Please tell me how to make these. (Mentioned by Alice Morse Earle as boys' pastimes.)
16. *Gum from the compass plant (rosinweed).* How do you gather this and what is the taste and texture of it? (Mentioned by Quinn, who says that Plains Indian children chewed this gum.)
17. How do you mold *milkweed pith* into toys?

Notes

Introduction

1. Or small pits in the ground would make,
And play at nuts, which he who lost,
His pleasure bitterly was crossed.
(Froissart, *L'Espinette Amoureuse* [1300s]. Quoted in Newell, p. 35.)

2. Plantain Duels: Gomme (1884) gives the names of the game and plant as follows.
   a) Cornwall: Cock-battler (hoary plantain)
   b) North (Suffolk): Cocks (ribwort plantain)
   c) West Sussex: Fighting Cocks (ribgrass)

   According to the Opies (1969) children called the plantain flower heads by the following names, depending on the region: Soldiers, Blackmen, Fighting Cocks, Hard-headed Knights, Carldoddies (in Perthshire), Kemps (in northern Scotland). (Old English *çempa*, a warrior; Middle English, *kempen*, to fight; Norwegian, *kjaempe* and *Swedish kämpa*, a plantain.)

Spring

1. The Chippewas, living on reservations in Minnesota, Wisconsin, and Ontario, Canada, gave information about their culture to Frances Densmore over an eighteen-year period, 1907 to 1925. Plate 51 in Densmore's book is a photograph of a duck (and two dolls) made from cattail leaves. (Since I have not been able to figure out how to make the ducks, I have listed them under Puzzlements.)

2. The pussy willow legend is retold from a version that appears in Méry. [According to Méry, the legend is Polish, but I have not been able to confirm its origin.]

3. "When we were in grammar school, each wooden desktop had an inkwell in the upper right-hand corner. Our compositions (the final drafts) had to be in ink. The teacher went around with a large bottle of ink — black or blue-black — with a spigot in the top. She put a small tube down into our inkwells, pressed a button, and filled them up." (Robert L. Chesanow, remembering William Cullen Bryant School in Great Barrington, Massachusetts, during the 1940s.)

4. Sébillot (1904) mentions the lucky lilac (one with five divisions of the floret), but not the swallowing ritual. (France, 1800s.)

5. Being "safe" while touching wood is related to the custom of knocking wood to protect against bad luck. Originally certain kinds of wood (oak, ash, hawthorn, apple, and willow) were thought to hold the most protection, but nowadays people touch the nearest wood or simply say "knock wood."

6. Maple seeds. Sébillot (1904) says that children let the seeds flutter to the ground, calling them butterfly wings or dragonfly wings. (France, 1800s.)

7. Sébillot (1904) describes numerous noisemakers made by children, including the dandelion stem horn. (France, 1800s.) He also mentions a horsetail stem whistle, as does Quinn. According to Quinn, Winnebago children made the horsetail whistles, but their parents would grab them away, cautioning the children that snakes would come in response to the sound.

8. Hottes (1949, p. 289) gives another version of the pansy story. Here is a summary:

   A fat king always sat on his throne with his feet stuffed into a green cushion to keep them warm. He had five daughters whom he wanted to keep with him always. The king got his wish because he and his daughters were changed into a pansy flower; the five petals are the girls and underneath is the little king.

More commonly, the story, which often is about a king, includes a stepmother. Beals (1917, p.57) ascribes the story to Scandinavia and Germany, where the pansy is known as the stepmother flower.

9. Sutton-Smith notes that little girls made Fairy Gardens, but does not elaborate. (New Zealand, 1900-1920s.)

10. The mertensia-doll story was recorded by Alice Morse Earle (1899, p. 384). Beals (1917, p.188) comments, "In colonial days the children were not permitted to play with toys on the Sabbath. But the little girls made dolls with red petticoats from the poppies."

11. Fernald (1958, p.76) said that "every country boy in New England and eastern Canada" looks for and eats the buckhorns even though the "nutty flavor" also has an "acridity" (which the small boys overlook).

12. Fernald and Kinsey (1958, p.143) mention that children call the cat brier by this name.

13. "Farmer boys of the northern states" gather the slivers of the inner bark of white pine in May and early June. (Fernald and Kinsey, 1958, p.77.)

14. According to Fernald and Kinsey (1958, p.154), the alder buds were popular nibbles to country boys less for their flavor than for the "beautiful, olive brown saliva produced."

15. The point that the early spring berries of wintergreen are more succulent than in the fall was made by Fernald and Kinsey (1958, p. 309).

16. Fernald and Kinsey (1958, p.161): "The tender young oak-apples or oak galls . . . contain a sweet juice . . . sucked out. . . . by children." Time is evidently the key element here. Spring is the time for sucking on the galls; later the juice can

be used for pretend paint and still later (fall?) the galls will be, as Coon says, "a perfectly round black-powder-filled ball." Coon, who calls the growths gall nuts, recommends the powder for making homemade ink.

17. According to Dana (1902, p. 50) the clammy azalea (or white swamp honeysuckle) has the "fleshy growths . . . which are so relished by the children."

18. Bergen (1899, no. 1383).

19. Bergen (1899) reports on the children digging the roots and giving them to neighbors. (New England, west to New York State, Ohio, and Kansas.)

20. In *Four Hedges* (Clare Leighton, Macmillan, 1932), Annie the housemaid is reminiscing about May Day in her girlhood. The following details are from her monologue:

    May Day used to be a school holiday in parts of England. The children would gather their flowers the day before, soak the garlands overnight, and go around to the houses the next morning, saying:

    Good morning ladies and gentlemen
    We wish you a happy day.
    We've come to show you our garlands
    Because it's the first of May.

    The flowers were both wild and cultivated, given to the children from people's gardens. The children wore the garlands and carried long poles trimmed with flowers; they would dress a favorite doll in white and put her atop two poles for the procession. Their chosen May Queen would have a special garland often topped with a crown imperial. The children called this flower Crown of Pearls because underneath the bloom you could see "pearls."

In the early 1800s children in New York city could be seen on the first of May, heading through the streets in groups bearing striped poles with ribbons streaming from the top, going to Central Park to continue the festivities — ring games,

games, songs, etc. ("Here we go 'round the mulberry bush, the mulberry bush . . . so early in the morning" is said to be a May Day singing game, the bush referring to the flowering branches that traditionally trimmed the houses.) (Newell, p.15, notes the New York children's May Day customs.)

21. Violet Fights. Bergen wrote an account of these contests for Newell's book, calling them a "ruthless" form of play and declaring, "I am glad to have known of a few little girls who were too humane to take part in this play." She adds that the pastime is common not only in the United States and Canada but also in Japan. A friend of Bergen's noted Native American children (at a summer encampment at York Beach, Maine) fighting with violets; the conqueror would be a great man, according to the children. Bergen also noted that the Onondagas have a name for violets meaning "two heads entangled," referring to this popular game.

22. Metcalf has abundant information on whistles — slip-bark whistles, a two-tone whistle, a slide trombone whistle. The simple willow whistle that everyone used to know how to make is also included. Other woods for this whistle that Metcalf recommends are striped maple (moosewood), dogwood, elder, poplar, viburnum, and basswood. In the southern states, bamboo makes a good whistle; in the north, Japanese knotweed, a large aggressive plant, has woody stalks that can make fine whistles. In fact, bamboo and knotweed whistles are easier to make than wood whistles because there's no bark to worry about. Just cut off a piece about four inches long, making the cut beyond a joint so the end will be plugged. Cut a notch in the top near the hollow end; insert a half-round plug in the hollow end, long enough to reach to the notch.

23. The buttercup story is adapted from a version that appears in Beals.

24. In Scotland in the 1800s, children also used the seed fluff

from the spear thistle to tell time by blowing on the seeds and counting the puffs. They called the flower Marion, and said:

Marion, Marion, what's the time of day?
One o'clock, two o'clock — it's time we were away.

(Thistleton-Dyer)

25. Quoted by Earle (1899, p. 380) and Beals (p. 39). Since no author was credited, I assume this was a traditional rhyme.

26. The name "pissabeds" originally referred to one of the plant's medicinal uses. Nicholas Culpepper prescribed dandelions as a remedy that effectively "openeth up urine," and commented that the plant was "vulgarly called pissabeds." Culpepper, a London physician, was the author of *The English Physician, or An Astrologo-Physical Discourse of the Vulgar Herbs of this Nation* (1692), a book used widely by both Britons and Americans during the seventeenth and eighteenth centuries. The name "pissabeds" appealed to youthful scatalogical humor and was retained long after the pharmaceutical use for dandelions had disappeared. (*Pissenlit* is the French common name for dandelion.)

Summer in the Garden

1. The seventeen-year (thirteen in the South) cicada is often called locust. After beginning life as an egg laid in a tree twig, the cicada hatches out a few weeks later as a nymph (small version of an adult) and immediately buries itself in the ground for the next seventeen (or thirteen) years. When it later returns to the surface, it sheds its skin (the source of toys).

2. According to Folkard (p.425), the ancient Romans ate mallow seed cases as vegetables, as did Egyptians, Syrians, and Chinese

3. Hollyhock dolls. Other people who wrote about making holly-

hock dolls were Doris Bisted (Ohio, 1930s), Margaret Drucker, Ginny Huggins, Lila Ritter (Kentucky, 1930s), Ann James van Hooser (Illinois, 1940s), Sally White (Meridian, New York, 1950s), Karen Taylor, Nancy Peiffer (Pennsylvania, late 1930s), Virginia York (Delavan, Wisconsin, 1940s), Jane Lynch (Ashville, Ohio, 1950s), Joy and Melody Smith (Wisconsin).

4. The poppies in the Morses' garden were probably opium poppies, which had been grown in this country since 1631. Although it is the gum of the seedheads that is processed to produce opium, the seeds themselves had been thought to be a sleep-causing drug. Galen, the second-century Greek physician, was contradictory in his writings on poppy seed, saying, on the one hand, that it was good to season bread, and, on the other hand, that "it causeth sleepe." Galen's philosophies were staunchly espoused by early American settlers, as Ann Leighton has shown, and well after Colonial days he was still revered by some. Thus the horrified elderly visitor to the Morse garden may have been voicing the opinion of a trusted authority such as Galen.

5. Sébillot (1904, p.191) also reports on poppy dolls (France, 1800s).

6. Pin-a-sights (poppy shows, pinny shows, pin dips, poppet shows). Gomme (England, 1800s) made her poppy shows just as Alice Earle did and called them poppy or poppet shows. She reported that the singsong words that accompanied the shows varied from place to place.

   A pin to see the poppet-show.
   All manner of colours, oh!
   See the ladies all below.
   (Gomme, recalling her own childhood, 1820s)

   From Sheffield:

   A pinnet a piece to look at a show,
   All the fine ladies sat in a row

Blackbirds with blue feet
Walking up a new street;
One behind and one before,
And one beknocking at t' barber's door.

And from Perth:

A pin to see a poppy show,
A pin to see a die,
A pin to see an old man
Sitting in the sky.

In Cheshire and Berkshire, the shows had colored pictures pasted inside and an eyehole at one end. From Leeds: "A pin to look in / A very fine thing."

Sutton-Smith (New Zealand, 1800s): "Girls had poppy shows, called more often Pin Dips. The words to entice the viewer went: 'A pin or a bull or a button / To see a rory rory show, show, show.'"

A *bull* was a marble. The *dip*, according to Sutton-Smith, was a "book or a glass front displaying pretty colors." (He does not mention flowers.) During the first decades of the twentieth century, Pin Dips remained popular, together with Prick Books (perhaps a commercial offshoot of Pin Dips). Each Prick Book contained postcards and pretty pictures. Each girl pushed a pin into the book and got to keep the picture on the page where her pin had pricked. When a fresh book appeared, its owner was deluged by friends who each wanted to be first to prick the book.

7. An unidentified friend of Bergen (United States, 1800s) supplied the information and the rhyme printed here. The shows varied with the seasons; the girls used apple blossoms, geranium petals, and many others in addition to the poppy petals. Bergen comments: "I should think likely that the show originally consisted of colored pictures or images of saints; it is popular etymology which has led to the use of poppies in America."

8. Author's note: The flower graves and sandbox peepshows

played in twentieth-century America seem to clearly be derived from poppy shows in the use of a decorative array of flowers covered over with glass and then displayed to friends. Since they were made in dirt, as the poppy shows were not, they may also be related to another English children's custom — grottoes. In some parts of London during late July (as recently as the 1960s, according to the Opies), children construct grottoes and ask for a penny to peek inside. To make a grotto, the children first put a pile of sand on a board (or on the pavement), then put tunnels through the pile, decorating them with bits of broken china and little stones. The outside might be covered with moss and flowers with a glass peephole to look in at the tunnels. A little pond (water in a jar lid) might also be a feature of a grotto. (Traditionally, a grotto was built with shells and was part of an oyster celebration, but "Grotter Day" continues without the shells.)

10. Turner, quoted in Folkard, p. 345.

11. According to Earle, the pumpkin-stem horns were made in the thirteenth century. Their sound is evidently piercing, since Thoreau noted in his journal (August 7, 1856): "Heard this forenoon what I thought at first to be children playing on pumpkin stems in the next yard, but it turned out to be the new steam-whistle music, what they call the Calliope (!) in the next town. It sounded more like the pumpkin stem near at hand, only a good deal louder."

Summer Afield

1. Pranks, Picking on Someone. The Opies (1969, p.198) list the following plant pranks: nettle walking (nettling), rubbing a dandelion on someone's face, putting itching powder down someone's back. ("Itching powder," or "itchy backs," was the soft center of unripe rose hips.) In a note on the same page they cite Edward Moor (born 1771) who commented

that it was common in his childhood to throw burs on girls' clothing or in a boy's or girl's hair. Shakespeare had Celia say: "They are but burs, cosen, thrown upon thee in holiday foolerie" *As You Like It* (1:iii) Sébillot reports on bur-throwing in Picardy and Upper Brittany (1800s) p.191.

Dock was known as a remedy for nettle burns back in Chaucer's time:

But kanstow pleyen raket, to and fro,
Nettle in, dokke out, now this now
That, Pandare?
(*Troylus and Creseyde*, iv, c. 1385.)

Children sometimes said rhymes when applying the dock leaf to the burn:

Out nettle, in dock
Dock shall have a new smock
But nettle shan't have nothing.
(*Encyclopedia of Superstition*)

or,

Out nettle, in dock
Dock shall have a new frock.
(Yorkshire, reported by Quinn, p. 74.)

2. Petal Pulling. *New Zealand:* Sutton-Smith mentions Grass Games in which each person pulls off the ears of the rye grass, saying, "He loves me, etc." *United States: The Journal of American Folklore,* vol. 31, 1918, gives a rhyme for daisy petal pulling, the same as the appleseed rhyme printed in the Autumn and Winter chapter of this book except for the last three lines, which are,

   Thirteen for riches
   Fourteen for stitches,
   Fifteen he tears a hole in his britches.
   That's what the daisies say.

3. Buttons. The Knapps (1978, p.255) add a third line to the "rich man, poor man" rhyme: "Tinker, tailor, cowboy, sailor." A grand mixture — the American cowboy inserted

among the traditional British occupations.

4. Clover. Hottes, p. 248, records this rhyme from Cambridgeshire:

   A clover, a clover of two
   Put it into your right shoe,
   The first man (woman) you meet,
   In the field, street, or lane.
   You'll love him (her) or one of his (her) name.

   Also:

   Find a two, put it in your shoe
   Three, let it be;
   Four, put it over the door;
   Five, let it thrive. [It's unlucky.]

   From Illinois, Hottes (p. 248) quotes this bit of lore: "Put a four-leaf clover in your shoe and get a buggy ride or a kiss."

   The Opies (1969, p. 23) quote Sir John Melton's *Astrologaster* (1620): "If a man, walking in the fields, finde any four leaved grasses, he shall in a small while after finde some good thing."

Autumn and Winter

1. Thoreau's journal, quoted by Dana (1902, p.193).
2. Willard Clute, long-time editor of *The American Botanist*, found a quote in one of the Maurice Thompson books: "[I] once went to school where everybody chewed sweet gum, except the teacher, who chewed tobacco." (Fernald and Kinsey, 1958, p. 228.)
3. Sébillot (1904, p. 63) says that in Upper Brittany in the sixteenth century children made popguns (pétoires) of elder. He mentions also syringes that shoot water. (Reported by Noël du Fail in 1547.)
4. Wild lettuce, a very tall plant (ten to twelve feet) of the north-

ern states, has hollow stems that make good blowguns when they become dry and stiff in the late fall. A straight section about four feet long with a top diameter (the far end of the blowpipe) of about one-third inch and a bottom diameter of about a half inch works well. It is best to cut the length and let it season for several weeks before using it.

Metcalf (chapter 7) tells how to make darts for a blowgun and describes several games: a balloon-breaking contest, "blow-fun golf," and "blow-fun for distance" — which will strengthen your lungs while you play. (Metcalf really knows his stuff and gives clear, detailed instructions for all the projects in his book — teachers and scout leaders, take note!)

5. A thorough history of Conkers, details of the game from opening words to strategies, and a description of the Conker madness that sweeps England every fall appear in the Opies' 1969 book on games.

6. Gomme, writing about London in the 1800s, reports a game called Ho-go, which she says is played with marbles (also called How Many Eggs in a Basket).

Player l. "Ho-go." (Holds up some marbles in his hand.)
Player 2. "Handful."
Player l. "How many?"

(Player 2 guesses some number. If the guess is exact, this player wins all the marbles; if the guess in lower than the actual number of marbles, this player must give the difference between his guess and the actual amount to Player 1.)

Alice Morse Earle (1898, p.139) mentions a game called Hull Gull How Many, which was played with dried corn kernels after the harvested corn had been stored away. Earle does not describe the game or give a source for the information, but it is safe to assume that it was the same game.

7. The word *philippine,* (also *fillipeen, fillipeener, Philippina,* and *philopena*) comes from the Greek *philos* (loving) and the Latin

poena (penalty), from the idea that the gift was a penalty of friendship or love.

The entry for *philopena* in Webster's Third: 1. A game in which a man and a woman who have shared twin kernals of a nut each try to claim a gift from the other as a forfeit at their next meeting by fulfilling certain conditions (as by being the first to exclaim *philopena*); 2a. a nut with two kernals; 2b. a gift given as a forfeit.

Newell (p. 113) uses *philopena* in its 2b sense to refer to a forfeit paid in a children's game, Green. In this game, played in the 1800s, one child would point at another and exclaim, "green!" which was the command to show a leaf, blade of grass, etc., or else pay a forfeit. Children often hid a leaf in their shoe or sock to fake being without green; when challenged, they would triumphantly pull out the bit of greenery (Georgia and South Carolina).

Both Philippine and Green were originally adult games of romance and intrigue. For example, the wealthy members of the French Sans-vert societies boisterously played Je Vous Prends Sans Vert (I Catch You Without Green), in which a common penalty was a dousing with a bucket of water (Newell and Sébillot).

8. Sébillot, p. 52: "In French-speaking Belgium, on the eve of St. Andrew's Day, young girls carefully peel an apple so that the peeling stays in one piece and throw it, without turning around, behind the headboard of the bed; the next day the peel will show a design which will be construed as the initial of the girl's future husband."

9. Sebillot, p. 51: "In French-speaking Belgium, a moistened appleseed which will stick to your forehead is a sign of true love. In Upper Brittany, boys who want to know where their sweetheart is, put appleseeds in their hand or in a hat and say,

   Pippin, pippin

Twist and turn
Because where the pippin points
My true love will be.

(The pointed end of the seed gives the answer.)

In The Hague young girls pop an appleseed from between two fingers, let it fall, and see which way it points. Their true love will come from that direction."

10. The Knapps (p. 254) note that the appleseed rhyme was in use in Mississippi in 1919. Sutton-Smith (1911) reports on this rhyme from Blenheim, Marlborough, New Zealand:

    Apple pip, apple pip
    Fly over my head
    Bring me another apple,
    Before I go to bed.

11. Folkard, p. 398, is the source of the cabbage (kale) predictions.
12. Geoffrey Charlesworth contributed the holly-leaf challenge, also a similar daredevil game with a nettle leaf. He wrote, "Grasp a nettle leaf firmly between finger and thumb; this prevents the sting — I suppose the hairs are compressed without penetration. The same thing with a holly leaf; it you grasp it firmly in the center of your palm and crush it, the thorny leaves don't penetrate." (Yorkshire, late 1920s.)
13. A jack-jumper gives one person an excitingly bumpy ride down a snow-covered hill. It is a wooden seat mounted on an upright metal bar attached to a runner curved up in front. You hold on to the sides of the seat and steer with your feet. [I remember boys bringing these to school for coasting during recess and lunch hour.] (Great Barrington, Massachusetts, 1940s.)
14. The maple icicles incident is based on the January twenty-ninth entry in Teale.

Common and Latin Names of Plants Described in Text

Reference: Hortus Third, *Liberty Hyde Baily (New York: Macmillan, 1976).*

acorn: *Quercus (fruit of)*
alder: *Alnus*
American chestnut: *Castanea dentata*
anise: *Pimpinella Anisum*
apple: *Malus*
aster: *Aster novae-angliae*
autumn clematis: *Clematis paniculata*
bachelor's button: *Centaurea cyanus*
balloons (children's name): *Sedum spectabile*
Balm of Gilead: *Populus balsamifera*
bamboo: *Arundinaria gigantea*
bamboo grass: *Arundinaria disticha* (?)
basswood: *Tilia americana*
bindweed: *Convolvulus arvensis*
birch: *Betula*
bird's eye: *Veronica Chamaedrys*
blackberry: *Rubus*
bladder campion: *Silene vulgaris (S. cuculabus)*
bleeding heart: *Dicentra spectabilis*
bloodroot: *Sanguinaria canadensis*
blowballs (children's name): *Taraxacum officinale*
blow leaf (children's name): *Sedum spectabile*
box(wood): *Buxus sempervirens*
bread and butter (children's name): *Smilax rotundifolia*
broad beans: *Vicia faba*
buckeyes: *Aesculus glabra*
buckhorns: *Osmunda cinnamomea*
burdock: *Arctium lappa*
butter and eggs: *Linaria vulgaris*
buttercup: *Ranunculus acris*
butternut: *Juglans cinerea*
cane: *Arundinaria gigantea*
canterbury bells: *Campanula*

medium

Carolina allspice: *Calycanthus floridus*

carrot: *Daucus carota*

cat brier: *Smilax rotundifolia*

cattail: *Typha*

cedar: *Juniperus virginiana*

checkerberry, checkermint: *Gaultheria procumbens*

cherry: *Prunus*

chestnut, American: *Castanea dentata*

chicory: *Chicorium intybus*

chinaberry: *Melia azedarach*

chinkapin (chinquapin): *Castanea pumila*

chokecherry: *Prunus virginiana*

cinnamon fern: *Osmunda cinnamomea*

citron: *Citrullus lanatus* var. *citroides*

clammy azalea: *Rhododendron viscosum*

clocks (children's name): *Taraxacum officinale*

clover, red: *Trifolium pratense*

clover, yellow sweet: *Melilotus officinale*

cock's foot: *Dactylis glomerata*

columbine: *Aquilegia*

corn: *Zea Mays* var. *saccharata*

cottonwood: *Populus deltoides*

creeping jenny: *Lysimachia Nummularia*

crown imperial (crown of pearls): *Fritillaria imperialis*

cucumber: *Cucumis sativus*

cudweed: *Gnaphalium obtusifolium*

Cupid's car: *Aconitum*

curly dock: *Rumex crispus*

daisy: *Chrysantheumum leucanthemum*

dandelion: *Taraxacum officinale*

devil's snuffbox: *Lycoperdon gigantea*

dock: *Rumex crispus*

dodder: *Cuscata gronovii*

dogtail grass: *Cynosurus cristatus*

dogtooth violet: *Erythronium americanum*

dogwood: *Cornus florida; Cornus kousa*

dragon root: *Arisaema triphyllum*

dutchman's breeches: *dicentra cucullaria*

elder: *Sambucus canadense*

elephant ear: *Colocasia*

English daisy: *Bellis perennis*

evening primrose: *Oenothera*

fairy folks' glove: *Digitalis purpurea*

fiddlehead: *Osmunda cinnamomea*

fig tree: *Ficus carioca*

filaree: *Erodium cicutariumn;*

Erodium moschatum
finger flower: *Digitalis purpurea*
flower de luce: *Iris*
four o'clock: *Mirabilis jalapa*
foxglove: *Digitalis purpurea*
frog bellies, frog plant (children's names): *Sedum spectabile*
fuchsia, California: *Fuchsia zauschneria*
fungus, bracket or shelf: *Basidiomycetes* group
fungus, scarlet cup-shaped: *Peziza* (?)
gardener's garters: *Pharalis arundinacea* var. *picta*
ginseng: *Panax quinquefolius*
golden seal: *Hydrastis canadense*
goldenrod: *Solidago*
gooseberry: *Ribes*
goosegrass: *Galium aparine*
grapevine: *Vitis*
ground cherry: *Physalis pruinosa*
hackberry: *Celtis laevigata*
hawthorn: *Crataegus*
hay-scented fern: *Dennstaedtia punctilobula*
hazelnut: *Corylus*
hickory: *Carya*
hoary plantain: *Plantago lanceolata*
holly: *Ilex aquifolium*
honesty: *Lunaria annua*
honeysuckle: *Lonicera japonica 'Halliana'*
horse chestnut: *Aesculus Hippocastanum*
horsetail: *Equisetum hyemale*
ivry-leaves: *Gaultheria procumbens*
jack-in-the-pulpit: *Arisaema triphyllum*
Japanese knotweed: *Polygonum cuspidatum*
jewelweed: *Impatiens capensis, I. pallida*
johnny-jump-up: *Viola tricolor*
johnson grass: *Sorghum halapense*
jonquil: *Narcissus jonquilla*
kapok (silk-cotton tree): *Ceiba pentandra*
ladies' delight: *Viola tricolor*
lady-in-the-bath, lady-in-a-boat: *Dicentra spectabilis*
lady's eardrops, lady's locket: *Dicentra spectabilis*
lady's slipper: *Cypripedium*
lady's sorrel: *Oxalis*
larkspur: *Consolida ambigua*
lieutenant's heart: *Dicentra spectabilis*
lilac: *Syringa vulgaris*
lily(pad), (waterlily): *Nymphaea odorata*
lily of the valley: *Convollaria*
lime-flower (lime tree): *Tilia cordata*
live-forever: *Sedum telephium*
lungwort: *Mertensia virginica*
lyre flower: *Dicentra*

spectabilis
mallow: *Hibiscus moscheutos*
mangel-wurzel: *Beta vulgaris, crassa* group
manzanita: *Arctostaphylus*
maple: *Acer*
marsh marigold: *Calthus palustris*
May apple: *Podophyllum peltatum*
meeting house flower: *Aquilegia*
memory root: *Arisaema triphyllum*
milkweed: *Asclepias syriaca*
money blower: *Taraxacum officinale*
money flower, money-in-both-pockets, money-seed: *Lunaria annua*
money wisher: *Taraxacum officinale*
monkshood: *Aconitum*
moosewood: *Acer pennsylvanicum*
mulberry: *Morus rubra*
mustard: *Brassica*
nasturtium: *Tropaeolum majus*
natal hay: *Tricholaena rosea*
nettle: *Urtica dioica*
night-blooming cactus (night-blooming cereus): *Selenicereus*
Norway maple: *Acer platanoides*
oak: *Quercus*. black (*Q. velutina*), red (*Q. rubra*), scarlet (*Q. coccinea*)
orpine: *Sedum telephium*
oxeye daisy: *Chrysanthemum leucanthemum*
palmetto, scrub: *Serenoa repens*
pampas grass: *Cortaderia*
pansy: *Viola* x *Wittrockiana*
parsley: *Petroselinum crispum*

parsnip: *Pastinaca sativa*
pawpaw: *Asimina triloba*
peach: *Prunus persica*
peanut: *Arachis hypogaea*
pear (seckel): *Pryus communis* "Seckel"
peas: *Pisum sativum*
pennywort: *Cymbalaria muralis*
peony: *Paeonia*
peppergrass: *Lepidium*
periwinkle: *Vinca rosea*
phlox: *Phlox paniculata*
picklebeds: *Taraxacum officinale*
pickles: *Rumex acetosella*
pine: *Pinus*. Norway (*P. resinosa*), pitch (*P. rigida*), red (*P. resinosa*), Scotch (*P. sylvestris*), white (*P. strobus*)
pinxter (pinxterbloom): *Rhododendron periclymenoides (R. nudiflorum)*
pissabeds: *Taraxacum*

officinale
plantain: *Plantago lanceolata, P. major*
pokeberry: *Phytolacca americana*
poplar: *Populus*
poppy: *Papaver orientale, P. somniferum, P. rhoeas*
potato: *Solanum tuberosum*
princess pine: *Lycopodium obscurum*
privet: *Ligustrum vulgare*
proud purse: *Calceolaria*
pudding-bag plant: *Sedum spectabile, S. telephium*
puffballs: *Lycoperdon gigantea*
puffer-bellies (children's name): *Sedum spectabile*
pumpkin: *Cucurbita*
pussy willow: *Salix discolor*
Queen Anne's lace: *Daucus carota*
quince (flowering): *Chaenomeles*
rabbit tobacco: *Gnaphalium obtusifolium*
radish: *Raphanus sativus*
ragged robin: *Lychnis flos-cuculi*
red sumac (scarlet sumac): *Rhus glabra*
ribbon grass: *Pharalis arundinacea* var. *picta*
ribwort plantain (ribgrass): *Plantago lanceolata*
rose: *Rosa.* apothecary, (*R. gallica 'officinalis'*), cabbage (*R. centifolia*), cinnamon (*R. cinnamomea*), rugosa (*R. rugosa*)
rose of Sharon: *Althea syriaca*
rye grass: *Secale cereale*
sarsaparilla, wild: *Aralia nudicaulis*
scarlet pimpernel: *Anagallis arvensis*
Scotch broom: *Cytisus scoparius*
scrub palmetto: *Serenoa repens*
sheeps shears (sheep sorrel): *Rumex acetosella*
shepherd's purse: *Capsella bursa-pastoris*
skunk cabbage: *Symplocarpus foetidus*
smokeballs: *Lycoperdon gigantea*
snapdragon: *Antirrhinum major*
snapweed: *Impatiens capensis, I. pallida, I. olivieri*
snowball: *Viburnum opulus*
sorrel: *Rumex acetosella*
sorrel, wood: *Oxalis acetosella*
Spanish moss: *Tillandsia usneoides*
spiderwort: *Tradescantia*
spring beauty: *Claytonia*

virginica
spruce: *Picea*
squash: *Cucurbita*
sticker burs: *Arctium lappa*
strawberry shrub: *Calycanthus floridus*
striped grass: *Pharalis arundinacea* var. *picta*
striped maple: *Acer pennsylvanicum*
sugar cane: *Saccharum officinarum*
sunflower: *Helianthus annuus*
swamp azalea (swamp honeysuckle): *Rhododendron viscosum*
sweetbrier; brier candy (children's name): *Rosa eglanteria*
sweet fern: *Comptonia peregrina*
sweet shrub: *Calycanthus floridus*
sweet pea: *Lathyrus odoratus*
syringa: *Philadelphus*
teaberry: *Gaultheria procumbens*
timothy: *Phleum*
touch-me-not: *Impatiens capensis, I. pallida*
trumpet vine: *Campsis radicans*
violet: *Viola*
violet wood sorrel: *Oxalis violacea*
Virginia bluebell (Virginia cowslip): *Mertensia virginica*
waterlily: *Nymphaea odorata*
weeping willow: *Salix babylonica*
wild lettuce: *Lactuca canadense*
wild sweet william: *Phlox divaricata*
willow: *Salix*
wintergreen: *Gautheria procumbens*
witches' bells: *Digitalis purpurea*
witch hazel: *Hamamelis virginiana*
yellow beet: *Beta vulgaris, crassa* group
yellow sweet clover: *Melilotus officinalis*
yellow wood sorrel: *Oxalis corniculata*
yew: *Taxus*
zucchini: *Cucurbita Pepo* var. *Melopepo* cv. 'Zucchini'

Bibliography

Books

Beals, Katharine (McMillan). *Flower Lore and Legend.* New York: H. Holland and Co., 1917.

Bergen, Fanny (Dickerson), ed. *Animal and Plant Lore; Collected from the Oral Tradition of English Speaking Folk.* New York: Houghton Mifflin and Co., 1899. (Published for the American Folklore Society.)

Coon, Nelson. *Using Wayside Plants.* New York: Hearthside Press, Inc., 1969.

Crowell, Robert. *The Lore and Legend of Flowers.* New York: Hayes and Rose, 1982.

Dana, Mrs. William Star. *How to Know the Wild Flowers.* New York: Scribner, 1902 (first edition, 1893).

Densmore, Frances: *How Indians Use Wild Plants for Food, Medicine, and Crafts.* New York: Dover Publications, 1974. (An unabridged re-publication of an Accompanying Paper, "Uses of plants by the Chippewa Indians," in Annual Report 44 of the Bureau of American Ethnology, Washington, D.C.: United States Government Printing Office, 1928.)

Doole, Louise Evans. *Herb and Garden Ideas.* New York: Sterling, 1964.

Earle, Alice Morse. *Child Life in Colonial Days.* New York: Macmillan, 1899.

______. *Old- Tme Gardens.* New York: Macmillan, 1901.

______. *Home Life in Colonial Days.* New York: Macmillan, 1898.

Emrich, Duncan. *The Whim Wham Book*. New York: Four Winds Press (Scholastic Press), 1975.

Fernald, Meritt Lyndon, and Alfred Charles Kinsey. *Edible Plants of Eastern North America*. New York: Harper, 1958.

Folkard, Richard, Jr. *Plant Lore, Legends, and Lyrics. Embracing the Myths, Traditions, Supersititions and Folk-lore of the Plant Kingdom*. London: Sampson Low, Marston, Searle, and Livingston, 1884.

Foley, Daniel J. *Toys Throughout the Ages*. Philadelphia: Chilton, 1962.

Haughton, Claire Shaver. *Green Immigrants: The Plants that Transformed America*. New York: Harcourt Brace Jovanovich, 1978.

Hottes, Alfred. *Garden Facts and Fancies*. New York: Dodd, Mead, c. 1949.

Gomme, Alice Bertha. *Traditional Games of England, Scotland, and Ireland*. New York: Dover Publications, 1964. (Reprint of the 2nd edition, 1884.)

Knapp, Mary and Herbert Knapp. *One Potato, Two Potato: The Folklore of American Children*. New York: W.W. Norton and Company, 1976.

Lacy, Allen. *Home Ground: A Gardener's Miscellany*. New York: Farrar, Straus & Giroux, 1984.

Leach, Maria, and Jerome Fried, eds. *Funk and Wagnall's Standard Dictionary of Folklore, Mythology and Legend*. New York: Funk and Wagnall, 1949-50.

Lehner, Ernst, and Joanna Lehner. *Folklore and Symbolism of Flowers, Plants and Trees*. New York: Tudor, 1960.

Leighton, Ann. *Early American Gardens "For Meate or Medicine."* Boston: Houghton Mifflin Company, 1970.

Méry, Fernand. *The Life, History and Magic of the Cat*. New York: Grosset and Dunlap, 1968.

Metcalf, Harlan G. *Whittlin', Whistles, and Thingamajigs*. Harrisburg, Pa.: Stackpole Books, 1974.

Newell, William Wells. *Games and Songs of American Children*. New York: Dover Publications, Inc., 1963. (An unabridged re-

re-publication of the 1903 edition of a work first published by Harper and Brothers in 1883.)

Newson, Elizabeth, and John Newson. *Toys and Playthings in Development and Remediation.* New York: Pantheon, 1979.

Olson, Sigurd. *Open Horizons.* New York: A. E. Knopf, 1969.

Opie, Iona, and Peter Opie. *Lore and Language of School Children.* London: Oxford University Press, 1959.

_______. *Children's Games in Street and Playground.* London: Oxford University Press, 1969.

Quinn, Vernon. *Leaves: Their Place in Life and Legend.* New York: Frederick A. Stokes Company, 1937.

Radford, E., and M. A. Radford. *Encyclopedia of Superstitions.* Edited and revised by Christina Hole. Chester Springs, Pa.: Dufour Edition, 1969.

Robinson, Cyril Edward. *Everyday Life in Ancient Greece.* London: Oxford, 1933.

Santmyer, Helen Hooven. *Ohio Town.* New York: Harper and Row, 1984.

Schenk, George. *The Complete Shade Gardener.* Boston: Houghton Mifflin, 1984.

Sébillot, Paul. *La Flore.* Paris: Guilmoto, 1904-6. (Paperback edition, Paris: Imago, 1985.) Passages quoted in *Honeysuckle Sipping* translated by J.R. Chesanow.

Sutton-Smith, Brian. *The Folk-games of Children.* Austin, Texas: University of Texas Press, 1972. (Published by The American Folklore Society.)

Teale, Edwin Way. *Circle of the Seasons.* Binghamton, N.Y.: Vail-Ballou Press, Inc., 1953.

Thistleton-Dyer, Thomas. *The Folk-Lore of Plants.* New York: Gale, 1968. (Reprint of 1889 edition.)

Treble, Henry A. *Everyday Life in Rome in the Time of Caesar and Cicero.* Oxford: Clarendon Press, 1958.

Wigginton, Elliot, ed. *Foxfire 3* (1975); *Foxfire 4* (1977); *Foxfire 6* (1980); Garden City, New York: Anchor (Doubleday).

Wright, Sally. *Gardening: A New World for Children.* New York: Macmillan, 1957.

Articles

Lauzon, Lorraine. "Fantasy Gardening." *The Paper: The Monthly Guide to the Berkshires and the Hudson Valley.* April 4-May 1, 1985.

Marmo, Christine. "Here's a Garden Flower That Can Be Sown on Snow." *New York Times*, January 26, 1986.

Naipaul, V.S. "Reflections of a Reluctant Gardener." *House and Garden*, January 1986.

Taylor, Hatsy. "Childhood Memories." *The Berkshire Eagle*, 19 Sept., 1986.

Index

PHOTO BY CHES

A NATIVE OF Great Barrington, Massachusetts, Jeanné Chesanow now lives in central Connecticut. Her description of life at home makes it clear that she is ever aware of small but important things:

"Cheshire, Connecticut, is a town set on several hills; I live on the side of one, looking west to another that changes color with the seasons. East of our house is the stately white Congregational church, whose bells I hear as I work in my garden. My writing literally moves to the beat of a different drummer, since the high school band practices daily just south of us.

"Most of my garden is free-form—three wavy peninsulas, one filled with the gray and silver plants I like—but the new herb garden is geometric, laid out in straight lines.

"My husband is a doctor who in his spare time grows hot peppers for his famous secret-recipe chili. We have two sons, Andrei and Matt, and a large orange cat, Marmalade. Since Marm keeps the garden free of mice and voles, I grow several kinds of catmint for him.

"While writing Honeysuckle Sipping, *I did many of the things that people wrote me about. I popped bladder campions, made pepper shakers out of poppy seed heads, stuck maple seeds to my nose — and, of course, I sipped honeysuckles."*